SELLING
TO VITO

SELLING
TO VITO
the Very Important Top Officer
3rd Edition

Get to the top. Get to the point.
Get the sale.

ANTHONY PARINELLO

Adams Media
New York   London   Toronto   Sydney   New Delhi

Adams Media
An Imprint of Simon & Schuster, Inc.
57 Littlefield Street
Avon, Massachusetts 02322

For information about special discounts for bulk purchases, please contact Simon & Schuster Special Sales at 1-866-506-1949 or business@simonandschuster.com.

The Simon & Schuster Speakers Bureau can bring authors to your live event. For more information or to book an event contact the Simon & Schuster Speakers Bureau at 1-866-248-3049 or visit our website at www.simonspeakers.com.

Manufactured in the United States of America

17 2021

Library of Congress Cataloging-in-Publication Data has been applied for.

ISBN 978-1-4405-0669-7
ISBN 978-1-4405-0734-2 (ebook)

HB 01.27.2021 1751

To my beloved mom, Josephine Rose, for her continued love and guidance—and for teaching me right from wrong.

And to my greatest raving fan, best friend, and mentor, my brother Al, who left this world too soon.

I will continually strive to make them both proud of me.

Contents

Acknowledgments

There are so many individuals whose hands, hearts and minds have touched this book. I am grateful to the entire team at Adams for their hard work and dedication; to the hundreds of VITOs who over the years have given me the knowledge and experience to continue to create meaningful intellectual work on this topic; to the over 2.5 million salespeople who have implemented this program, who continue to follow my advice, and who push me to continual self-improvement . . . so the teacher can stay one step in front of the student; to my editor, Brandon Toropov, for his incredible ability to read my mind and who's been with this project since the writing of the first edition in 1993; and to my team at VITO Central: Beth Allen, Miki Davis, John Sell, Heather Burke, and Kim Barnett, who at times seem to know me and my work better than I do. I also want to express my thanks to my family and my many friends who have contributed to this book in ways large and small over the years. Finally, I want to thank you, the reader; without you, there would be no book at all!

Foreword

I first ran into VITO Selling in 2003, when I was working as a sales-person—and I quickly realized that it was designed to deliver exactly what I was trying to make happen in my own sales career: high-level contact, a truly consultative approach, and aggressively shortened sales cycles. All three became realities in my own career. I did, well, eventually become a CEO . . . and built the VITO program into the sales "DNA" of Sterling Commerce.

Based on my own personal experience, and the results we've seen at Sterling Commerce, I believe the relationships you create by deploying the VITO tactics and philosophy can drive double-digit or even greater levels of sales growth. That's regardless of the state of the economy and regardless of the state of your particular industry. These kinds of dramatic increases played out for us consistently over a four-year period. They are solely the result of improved sales efficiency.

VITO selling can change your career, just as it did mine. And it can certainly transform your sales team. What follows works. Use it!

Bob Irwin, CEO, Sterling Commerce

Prologue: Altitude and Attitude

When I saw him, I was in northern Washington State, waiting for a ferry to take me across the water to Vancouver Island in British Columbia.

In the middle of a six-city speaking tour, I had decided to drive to the island rather than fly from Seattle. My ferry's departure was still thirty minutes away, and I was sitting on the dock, taking in the beautiful scenery and daydreaming, when I saw him approaching the shoreline: some kind of bird. Considering the distance this bird was covering, he didn't seem to be flapping his wings very often. As he sailed closer and closer to me, I realized that I wasn't just looking at "a bird," but at a bald eagle in full flight.

He was huge, with a wingspan that seemed impossible. He was majestic. And for a moment, he left me literally breathless.

As he drew closer and closer to me, he dipped toward the water then banked upward gracefully, gaining altitude quickly as he landed, perfectly and without the slightest instability, flutter, or hesitation, on the top of a telephone pole in front of my car.

I grew up as an inner-city kid in Hoboken, New Jersey. I can spot a pigeon a mile away, but I had never, ever seen a real, live, *soaring* bald eagle until that day in 1993. As he sat on the top of that pole, the eagle scanned the water, looking for his next opportunity. Somewhere just beneath the surface, an unsuspecting fish was about to become breakfast.

I stared at him until it was time to get on the ferry. He never stopped scanning the water.

Lots of research has been done on the bald eagle, America's national bird. As it turns out, when eagles fly they almost always fly alone. You will never see a flock of bald eagles. When they land somewhere, they almost always land on the highest available spot. It could be a branch, a perch, an outcropping, or, as in this case, a telephone pole. Do you know why they land on the highest spot? Well, first of all, they aim for it. And second, because that's the position from which they can see everything that matters to them: the landscape, their prey, and any predators they may have to deal with.

Bald eagles prefer to fly alone. They like the vantage point they get from the top. They maintain a certain altitude and a certain attitude. In fact, just from watching that one eagle at close range, I came to my own conclusion about the altitude, and attitude, of bald eagles.

That day, I realized that bald eagles not only enjoy being at the top . . . they feel they DESERVE to be at the top. That eagle reminded me of someone who was already very familiar to me—someone who is about to become very familiar to you, too. I call that someone VITO: The Very Important Top Officer.

Introduction

Hello! It's me, Tony Parinello, the creator of VITO Selling. As you know, this is the third edition of *Selling to VITO: The Very Important Top Officer*. I am proud to say that I've rewritten the book from beginning to end to bring it up to date for selling in the twenty-first century!

The sub-title of the book says it all: *Get to the top. Get to the point. Get the sale.* And that's exactly why you'll find the basic methodology of *Selling to VITO* is unchanged. Everything you'll read here is still based upon my own continued selling experiences with CEOs, presidents, and owners of small, mid-market, and mega F-100 global enterprises—as well as on my teaching and mentoring of more than 2.5 million salespeople representing every possible product you can think of.

Over the past years, I've gotten a lot of pressure from salespeople to water down my core principle that whatever you sell, you're better off connecting with the office of the president, CEO, or founder of the enterprise before talking to anyone else. I can't count the number of salespeople who have debated this point with me, insisting that people with those titles simply don't buy what the company sells—

be it office supplies, cleaning supplies, copiers, computers, software, pharmaceuticals, whatever. Most of these sellers felt they sold a commodity or something of no interest to VITO, that VITO just didn't care about that kind of purchase. Over the past twenty-two years, I've held the line on my gut feeling and my personal VITO selling experience, which is that VITO cares about the *results* of anything and everything sold to VITO, Inc.

Guess what? I was right! After more than two decades of field testing, I've proven beyond a shadow of a doubt that VITO *does* care, VITO *does* decide quickly, and VITO does *buy* every single item whose results can help in the overachievement of VITO's goals. Not only does VITO buy—VITO buys big!

My job is to teach you how to position yourself as the dominant provider of value . . . VITO-style. To do that, I am going to ask you to change the way you look at yourself, your product, your marketplace, your organization, and your selling style. If you're ready for a challenge—and the rewards that accompany meeting that challenge— you've come to the right place!

At this point, you may be thinking: "Wait a minute, Tony. Rewrite or no rewrite, by the time I buy this book, it's already going to be old! After all, it's ink on paper, and that means it was fresh when you wrote it but not while I'm reading it!" That's where technology comes in. As a reader of this book, you're cordially invited to participate in a special live weekly Internet broadcast called *Club VITO*, with yours truly behind the microphone. I'll keep you up to date on all of the VITO selling tactics, and I'll answer all your market-specific questions as they come up during your implementation of this program. To learn how to access your free initial subscription to *Club VITO,* just flip to the last page in this book.

So, if you find yourself getting stuck on anything that follows, don't give up! Instead, join in and participate in *Club VITO*, and I'll coach you through whatever challenge you're having.

It's time to Think, Sell, and Live Large,

Tony Parinello

P.S. Before you move on, I'd like to make a promise to you. What you're about to learn in the pages and chapters that follow is what I use in my own sales process. The day I stop using my work myself to get appointments and sell to VITO is the day I'll stop writing books about it, teaching seminars about it, and hosting Club VITO. Rest assured that everything I teach you to do I also do myself. I also promise you that everything I ask you to do will be ethical and will not cost you any sleep at night.

Chapter 1

Meet VITO,
the Very Important Top Officer

In your current sales approach, how high up the corporate "org chart" do you land on your initial call or contact? Are you typically starting at the very top of the organization chart or are you more likely to be starting on the first or second branch from the bottom of that chart, with the lower-level supervisors/buyers/managers/purchasing agents/associates?

Most of the salespeople I work with are a little uneasy about answering this question directly at first. They hem and haw and talk about what happened when they once called on a CEO, president, owner, or other "C"-level executive. I'm not asking who you eventually meet; I'm asking who you typically start your sales process with.

I believe you *must* answer this question forthrightly if you are to benefit in any way from what follows in this book. Be honest with yourself: *Who have you been calling on and selling to?* Write the actual titles of the *ten* most recent *new* contacts you have called on in the space on the following page.

Titles of People You've Called On	
Name	*Title*

Where Are You on the "Org Chart"?

I want you to look very carefully at the titles of the people you've recently been trying to sell to, and then, if you dare, I want you to ask yourself one critical question that can literally transform your selling career if you are willing to ponder the answer carefully enough.

What kind of flooring were these people standing on?

When you met with these folks to talk with them about your product, service, or solution, were you standing on solid mahogany?

Was there deep, comfortable plush carpet everywhere you walked? Was there imported, inlaid marble at your feet? Were you walking down the aisle of someone's private jet? Well, if you wrote titles like "Buyer" or "Admin" or "Purchasing Director" in the preceding spaces, I'm guessing the answers to these questions about flooring were "no."

In fact, I'm going to guess that you were standing on *linoleum.*

Yep. If you're like most of the people I've taught over the years, you were standing on cheap flooring . . . with someone who kept putting off decisions. Someone whose life's mission was making you jump through hoops. Someone who always wanted to *see more* from you—more samples, more demos, more references, more advice, more meetings, more whatever.

I'm betting that no matter what you offered, no matter how many good ideas you brought to the table, that "buyer" (and notice the quote marks around that word) standing on linoleum with you did an awful lot of procrastinating and not much actual deciding or buying. The process dragged out. And if you ended up getting any business, you didn't get as much as you deserved.

Am I right?

I thought so.

Wasting Away Again in Linoleumville

You know how I knew? Because years ago, while I was a young(er) salesperson working for Hewlett-Packard, I used to start my sales cycle in Linoleumville—just like you're doing right now. I spent most of my day (heck, months!) talking to the "Seemores," (I'll explain that interesting word shortly) who dragged out my sales cycle, put off decisions, and restricted my access to others in the organization. Sound like anyone you know?

Because I was full of ambition and energy and competitive spirit, I made that sales process work—for a while. I was named Hewlett-Packard's Rookie of the Year in my division. Then, after several years of being at the top, I got complacent. I stopped prospecting; I started coasting. And I woke up one morning to find myself miles and miles and miles behind quota, staring at a memo from my boss informing me that I was officially on probation. I had just six months to turn things around—or lose my job.

Well, I didn't want to lose my job, so I started thinking: *What the heck can I possibly do to hit quota within the next six months?* A little voice inside told me that if I kept wasting my time in Linoleum-ville, I didn't stand a chance.

I listened to that little voice, and thank God I did, because once I started listening, I started calling at the top of the organization. It was at this fateful point in my career that I started Selling to VITO.

You can probably guess the end of the story. I hit my yearly quota, much to the astonishment of my manager. And I started the next year with a new perspective. Now that I had figured out a way to close bigger deals, quicker, what was I going to do—go back to calling the "Seemores" of the world? No way!

I didn't realize it then, but in closing that gap by the end of the year, I had harnessed the power of something I now call the *Network of Influence and Authority*. This is a helpful structural breakdown that is a) common to virtually all enterprises and b) great for accelerating your sales cycle and increasing your average order size . . . *if and only if* you are willing to start at the top of the Network.

Take a look at the four players in the Network briefly right now. Don't worry if the labels seem strange to you initially; you'll be getting to know each of these four folks very well in the pages that follow. Notice who occupies the topmost perch!

The Influence and Authority Network

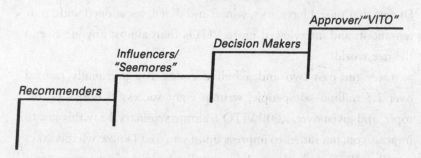

Meet VITO, the Very Important Top Officer

Remember that telephone pole my eagle landed on? How many tops did it have? That's right: one. If that telephone pole represented the corporate "org chart," the very top of it is where you would find the main character of this book: VITO!

Why is VITO at the top? Because, like an eagle, VITO intentionally aimed for it! Because, from the top, VITO can see everything that's critically important! Because VITO has responsibility for all that lies below. Because VITO has the ultimate *veto* power over absolutely everything that happens in the organization.

Believe it: VITO is the one person who is the *most* interested in the economics of the organization, the growth of the organization, the compliance of the organization, the you name it of the organization. Heck, VITO *is* the organization!

VITO RULE #0	(The rule from which every other VITO Rule is derived!): VITO is the ultimate approver of everything that happens in the organization, including your sale.

VITO is the person I've been selling to for the past three decades. During that time, I have, met, wined and dined, vacationed with, written about, and interviewed more VITOs than almost anyone else in the free world!

Over the past two and a half decades, I've personally trained over 2.5 million salespeople, written eight successful books on the topic, and given over 3,000 VITO training seminars. I say this not to impress you, but rather to impress upon you that I know what it takes to sell to VITO. I also know how to tell whether a salesperson really possesses the mindset necessary to take what I teach and take action on it. As you'll find out in the chapters that follow, having the proper state of mind is an important part of what it takes to sell to VITO.

Are *you* ready to sell to VITO? Go on to the next chapter to find out.

Chapter 2

Are You Ready to Sell to VITO?

Sometimes, people tell me they don't think they're "ready" to sell to VITO. Fortunately, I've developed an effective, quick, and painless method for determining whether a salesperson really has what it takes to sell to VITO. You're about to take advantage of that method. For the next few paragraphs, I want you to absorb three "VITO Insights," and then, once you've internalized what you've read, give honest answers to the questions that follow. Ready?

 **You have more in common with VITO than you think.**

ALL ABOUT VITO

For starters, VITOs have *big egos!* A healthy ego is a defining trait of high achievers, and it's certainly a defining trait among VITOs.

What else? *Power, control, and authority* are important to VITOs.

VITOs are *brief, direct, and to the point.*

VITOs are *self-assured, self-determined, driven to success,* and *goal and results oriented.*

VITOs are highly *accountable;* they are used to accepting responsibility.

VITOs are *passionate* and *highly competitive;* they love to win and hate to lose.

VITOs are *seekers of information that will give them an edge.*

VITOs are constantly on the lookout for ideas that will help them *over-accomplish their goals, plans, and objectives.*

VITOs *live in a time-compressed world.* They have learned, from personal experience, the importance of investing their precious time with people they feel will help them quickly prosper.

VITOs are *well read, well informed, and highly knowledgeable about the industry in which they're operating.*

For the most part, VITOs have an *"early adopter" mentality;* they spend time looking for good ideas that no one else has yet embraced.

VITOs are *risk takers* and *straight shooters.* They like being asked direct questions and they like individuals who will give them direct answers to the questions *they* ask.

Take a moment and reread the material in that box carefully. READ RIGHT OUT LOUD all of the words and phrases that are in *italics*. Do this before you move on in this book.

Okay, here comes your first question.

How many of the VITO traits, characteristics, and attitudes you just read out loud do you have?

If your answer was two or fewer, give this book to someone else. Not only should you not be selling to VITO, you probably should not be in sales.

If your answer was three or more, you've found the right book! There's no real surprise here. According to current research (and my own personal experience), something like 85 percent of all VITOs were once salespeople! They made cold calls, faced rejection, probed for needs, got put off, lost deals, and maybe even got put on probation. They went for the close. They made the sale. They lost the sale. They did it all, just like you and me! The remaining 15 percent or so, who didn't come up through sales, know the importance of sales. The old "Nothing happens until something is sold" adage certainly applies in VITO's world—just as it does in yours.

You may not have the title of a VITO, but you are very much *like* VITO. Think about this: If we were to catalog the traits, characteristics, and attitudes of the people you are currently trying to sell to, how many traits would you have in common with those individuals? My guess is few or none. What does this tell you? Here's what it tells me:

1. You're spending time trying to sell to individuals with whom you have little or nothing in common.
2. You're trying to sell to individuals who are less informed, less empowered, and less likely to make any decision at all. Where VITO embraces intelligent risk and makes clear decisions when confronted with risk, many others in VITO, Inc. want

nothing whatsoever to do with risky situations and consider virtually all decisions to be risky!

3. While you're spending time with people other than VITO, assume that your competition may well be reaching out to VITO . . . and that's not a good thing for you or your organization.

Let's face it: Whoever gets to VITO first, wins—because VITO can say yes and make it stick, and say no and make it stick. That's what having the ultimate veto power is all about.

VITO INSIGHT

#2   VITOs need what you have.

Picture VITO driving to work early in the morning in a high-powered luxury sedan. What do you suppose VITO is thinking about during that drive?

I know the answer to that question. I've recorded the key points from several decades of interviews with hundreds of VITOs in a series of personal journals. The more VITOs I sold to, the more journal entries I made about the goals, plans, and objectives that drove them. I analyzed the journal entries closely and made two critical discoveries:

1. VITOs in similar industries have similar goals, plans, and objectives.
2. VITOs in *all* industries share the same basic "short list" of critical goals, plans, and objectives.

Once you know what's on the "short list," you can connect with a VITO in virtually any industry; that is, if you can offer something that appeals to an item on VITO's "short list."

Here is VITO's "short list:"

1. Increasing revenues and exceeding the projected revenue plan
2. Increasing efficiencies and effectiveness of:
   » Revenue-generating employees
   » Mission-critical employees
   » Mission-critical processes
   » Workflow and related operations
   » Procurement
   » Capital resources
   » Customer-facing services
3. Cutting and or containing costs and moving away from unpredictable expenses and toward accurate, forecasted budgets.
4. Staying in compliance; operating well within the corporate culture on critical decisions; staying on the right side of all relevant governmental regulations and the law.

With this list in mind, let's focus for a moment on the product, services, and solutions you sell, thinking more about the "hole" and not at all about the "drill bit." What result(s) do you have a record of delivering or do you suspect your product, service, or solution can deliver that connects to each of the results listed above? Don't rush through this question. Take your time. Use the following "mind joggers" to help you get started:

Spend a minimum of ten minutes on each of these:
1. How does what I sell impact top line revenues?
2. How does what I sell impact the efficiencies of direct sales, online sales, brand awareness, marketing, operations, finance, manufacturing, customer service?
3. How does what I sell help contain or cut costs?

4. How does what I sell assist in compliance operations, keeping people and organizations out of legal trouble?

The big question: Of the four results where all VITOs want to overachieve, how many can your product, service, or solution help them with?

If your answer was, *"None"* or *"Gee, I don't really know,"* then you have a choice. Either look at this question a little more closely (I'll help you out with that in just a second) or give this book to someone else who can benefit from it.

• • •

Still with me? Great!

*If you said the answer to **the big question** was "None" or "I don't know," you almost certainly did not spend enough time completing the mind-jogger exercise. No problem. All you have to do to rectify the situation is conduct the following simple mental exercise:*

Picture the VITO of your very best account. Picture that person very happy. Whatever you've delivered is working flawlessly and life is good. VITO, Inc. continues to order all sorts of stuff from you.

Now imagine that at the stroke of midnight, a very strange situation takes place—every product, service, and solution you sold to Mr. Benefito does a sudden, mysterious disappearing act. Absolutely everything you ever sold into this account is vanished, gone, nowhere to be found. At 8:00 A.M. today, as the worker bees settle into their workstations, they have to go through the entire day without your stuff!

Now answer this question: In this situation, what would happen to Mr. Benefito's company? Write the answer to that question on your shower wall, carve it on your car's dashboard, have it tattooed down your right arm . . . whatever you need to do to constantly remind yourself of the contribution you make to VITOs' overachievement of their goals, plans, and objectives in the four short-list areas. Here they are again:

1. Increasing revenues and exceeding the projected revenue plan
2. Increasing efficiencies and effectiveness of:
   » Revenue-generating employees
   » Mission-critical employees
   » Mission-critical processes
   » Workflow and related operations
   » Procurement

- » Capital resources
- » Customer-facing services
3. Cutting and or containing costs and moving away from unpredictable expenses and toward accurate, forecasted budgets
4. Staying in compliance; operating well within the corporate culture on critical decisions; staying on the right side of all relevant governmental regulations and the law

Chances are you could answer yes (with specific examples) to at least three of the four elements. If you didn't, you may want to go to an online job site and submit an updated resume! If you're working for an organization that can't deliver in at least three of these areas, they will almost certainly be out of business within the next few months.

VITOs need what you have. VITO is waiting for you to show up with a letter, e-mail, fax, telephone call, voice mail message, Tweet, Facebook entry, or your old-fashioned smiling face in his or her lobby.

VITO INSIGHT #3 You are VITO.

Every sales job comes with expectations. It's been my personal experience that most of these expectations tend to spin around such issues as territory development, quota performance, effective use of your resources, team playing and "professionalism," and compliance with the sales process and the corporate culture of the enterprise you happen to be selling for.

If you stop and think about it, you will realize that the expectations you are responsible for boil down to these four:

1. Revenue generation
2. Effectiveness/efficiency/resource management
3. Cost and time containment
4. Compliance

Look familiar? It should.

You and VITO are measured in pretty much the same basic ways. Sure, you can argue about some small differences, but the big point is what's worth noticing: What VITO wants to accomplish at VITO, Inc. is what you want to accomplish for yourself and the organization you sell for.

Read it again.

What VITO wants to accomplish at VITO, Inc. is what you want to accomplish for yourself and the organization you sell for.

Ask yourself: Would you spend time with someone with whom you shared similar traits, characteristics, and attitudes . . . who had goals, plans, and objectives that were similar to yours . . . and who had the possibility of bringing ideas to the table that would help you overachieve your goals, plans, and objectives?

If your answer was, *"No, not really,"* then schedule a vacation. Clearly, you've been working too hard.

Let's look at where we are so far. VITO sits at the top or the organization and has the ultimate veto power. VITO's traits and your traits are quite similar. The results VITO wants to achieve with his or her organization and the results you want to achieve in your own sales career are quite similar, and the results your product can deliver are potentially in alignment with what VITO needs to ensure overachievement at VITO, Inc.

Once you've processed all that, say these VITO Rules out loud:

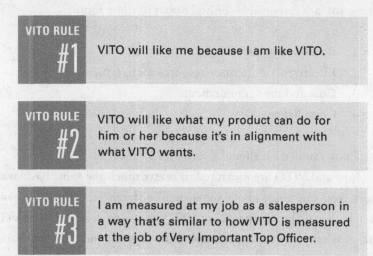

VITO RULE #1
VITO will like me because I am like VITO.

VITO RULE #2
VITO will like what my product can do for him or her because it's in alignment with what VITO wants.

VITO RULE #3
I am measured at my job as a salesperson in a way that's similar to how VITO is measured at the job of Very Important Top Officer.

You are now officially READY to sell to VITO.

Chapter 3

Spotlight on the Sales Process

After selling and training for over thirty years in the Fortune 100, and after consulting with more than 5,000 mid-market selling organizations over the same period, I am in a position to tell you what amounts to a closely guarded inside secret. Ready?

About 70 percent of those companies I worked with initially either had NO clearly defined selling process or had a process mapped out but didn't follow it.

What does that have to do with VITO, you, and *your* sales performance this year, month, or quarter? *Everything!*

The big point is that ideas and tactics you will encounter in *Selling to VITO* will "plug and play" seamlessly with your current sales process (if you have one)—or *serve* as your sales process if you haven't had one set up for you or identified for yourself what your sales process ought to be. Before we go any further, let's define a sales process:

A *sales process* is a series of sequential steps taken over some quantifiable period of time. When these steps are followed, they convert *suspects* (people you have not sold to yet, but want to) into *prospects* (people who are talking to you about buying your stuff) into *customers* (you know what those are), yielding a completed sale that puts commission dollars in your purse or pocket and delivers revenue to the top line of the company you work for.

Let me offer a few words of caution: There is a big difference between your sales process and your sales forecast. An accurate sales forecast is a result of having an effective sales process . . . and *using* it.

How about you and your sales process? Are you actually using one? Do you have one that you know is workable but don't use it? Are you selective about the steps you use? As we move forward here, I'm going to challenge you to assume accountability for four action steps, all of which relate to your sales process. As you assume accountability for each, please avoid the temptation to say (or think), "Hey, that's not my job." Believe it or not, all four actions have always been part of your job. The four steps are:

Step One: Create your sales process
Step Two: Analyze your sales process
Step Three: Improve your sales process
Step Four: Replicate your sales process (as quickly as possible!)

Now, let's look once again at our agreed-upon definition of a sales process. Here's the opening sentence of the definition, which I'd like you to read out loud right now:

A *sales process* is a series of sequential steps taken over some quantifiable period of time.

I'd like to draw your attention to one particular word in that sentence that is critically important: *time*.

In VITO's world (and in yours and mine), time is a precious resource. It may well be the ultimate resource. You and I must always respect the value of that resource in our approach to VITO as far as our interactions, written correspondence, telephone, in-person meetings, and all of our follow-up is concerned. It's been my experience that if I respect time in my own world (which by definition includes all of my sales work), it's a heck of a lot easier for me to understand and respect the value of time in VITO's world.

Countless studies have been made about how to save time or increase the speed of various business operations that require time so that a given outcome (for instance, a product, service, or sale) can be produced while reducing investments of time. Increasing the velocity of a process during some specific timeframe is also a very popular activity. Examples include speed-to-revenue and speed-to-results for the enterprise and the speed-to-commission we as salespeople can enhance by accelerating our own sales process. Not to mention speed-to-decision, which is a function of knowing where to spend and invest our time and with whom we should be spending and investing it with.

VITO RULE #4 Because time is so valuable, VITOs don't treat all potential business relationships equally, and neither should you.

Your time, your organization's resources, and your revenue forecasts must reflect your most intelligent use of time with various people in different business relationship categories. Identifying and understanding the individual elements of your organization's current sales process means identifying the various groups that make that process possible. They fall into six possible categories.

Six Important Categories

1. *Suspects* are individuals or organizations who fit some prequalification filter or list of criteria, whether that's a profile developed by your marketing department or your own quantified set of

criteria, which I call the Template of Ideal Prospect (T.I.P.), about which you'll hear more in an appendix at the end of this book.

2. *Prospects* are those individuals or companies that have already been contacted by some method and who comply with the criteria necessary to become customers, business partners, and/or distributors and whom you are currently in a dialog with. The key word here is "currently." Most salespeople have a fairly loose definition of a prospect; some actually consider a prospect to be "Anyone I spoke to over the past six months about the possibility of working with us."

3. *Customers* currently buy from you. Here again, the key word is "currently." Most salespeople have a fairly loose definition of a customer; some actually consider a customer to be "anyone who ever bought anything from us." VITOs, however, know that a customer is someone who is providing contributions to the top line and doing so right now. Use VITO's definition of a customer over any other.

4. *Business partners* not only buy from you currently but also prosper from their relationship with you in a way that clearly surpasses what your product, service, or solution does for them. That means, for instance, that you might share critical knowledge, strategic resources, leads, prospects, or even customers with business partners for mutually beneficial reasons.

5. *Distributors* are individuals or organizations that take your products, services, and/or solutions, add some kind of direct or indirect value, and maybe even take your name off and put theirs on and resell it.

6. *Advocates* can also fall into one or more of the above categories. This is an individual or organization eager to see you succeed in your sales efforts and willing to help you sell. Over the years, advocates have also been called "inside coaches" or "sponsors."

Reality Check

Take a moment and, in the space below do a reality check on your sales forecast. List the primary contacts and their titles in the top ten selling opportunities in your "pipeline" as of today. Categorize everyone who is *currently* in your sales forecast against the definitions above, then write what you come up with in the boxes below:

#	Suspect	Prospect	Customer	Contact	Title
1					
2					
3					
4					
5					
6					
7					
8					
9					
10					

Once you have completed that activity, move on to the next chapter.

Birds of a Feather

What did you find out? What kind of *titles* are actually connected to the income you are forecasting from your pipeline?

---

*I have a more rigorous definition of "prospect" than most sales systems suggest. For practical purposes, a prospect is someone who is in active discussions with you about buying, has communicated with you in the last week, and returns your calls within forty-eight hours.

Were most of your sales opportunities in that third category— *customers* who are already buying from you? Or were *prospects** the most numerous category?

Is it possible that you are forecasting most of your income from *suspects*—people you have targeted, but with whom you have not yet established any selling discussion? What about *business partners* and *advocates?* How many of those are visible on your landscape?

Here's what a healthy mix would look like for most of the "hunter" salespeople I work with. If your job is something other than hunter— for example, if you have a territory of installed accounts—keep reading, and consider what follows a case study.

TARGET PIPELINE NUMBERS

Suspects = 0 percent (They don't belong in your sales forecast.)

Prospects = 75 percent

Customers (including Business Partners and Distributors) = 25 percent

Advocates = 50 percent or greater (Remember, Advocates overlap the other categories; they're your cheerleaders within the buying enterprise. When I say 50 percent of your opportunities or greater should be advocates, I mean that at least half of your Prospects and at least half of your Customers should have a strong Advocate within the organization who's helping you.)

Now it's time for a tough question: *How close does your sales pipeline come to matching this standard?*

What Would VITO Do?

Pop quiz: Who would *VITO* spend time with? What kinds of people would VITO reach out to first? Let's say that a CEO, president, or owner of one of the companies you sell to had to make a sales call that was designed to turn a suspect into a prospect—which, by the way, is not at all rare. Whom do you think VITO would call? What title do you think VITO would set up a meeting with? If you answered another VITO, give yourself a gold star! There is just no doubt about it: VITO would call another VITO. Let's say for a moment that VITO had to make a sales call on an existing customer. Again, it happens more often than you may think. What title do you think VITO would reach out to? Right again: VITO! Now let's say that VITO wanted to find, develop, and nurture a relationship with an Advocate. What title do you think VITO would reach out to? Is there a pattern emerging here? Of course—VITO would call another VITO! I guess it's true: Birds of a feather really do flock together! Which bird did we decide you wanted to fly with again? Right! VITO—the eagle! So, just out of curiosity, how many VITOs are in *your* current sales forecast? If you're like most of the salespeople I work with, the titles currently in your sales forecast probably don't include many VITOs—not yet anyway.

Here are some titles and numbers from the combined sales forecasts of a sales team I worked with over a ninety-day period.

What Specific Job Titles Are in Our Sales Forecast?		
Title	Before Selling to VITO	After Selling to VITO
Purchasing Agent	2,111	2,111
Buyers	389	389
Managers	140	140
Directors	21	21
Vice Presidents	8	600
"C" Suite	58	97
President	0	152
CEO	0	38
Owner	10	16

Look at the numbers above; notice that *none* of the relationships at lower levels were sacrificed! The true definition of Selling to VITO means that you proactively engage VITO without ignoring any other players.

VITO RULE #5 When you fly with VITO, everybody else in the organization follows!

No Cop-Outs

If you want to make your sales process work more effectively—and by that I mean make it deliver bigger sales and bigger commission checks to you in shorter amounts of time—you have come to the right chapter. Here is where you'll learn exactly how to pull that off:

> *Be personally accountable for each and*
> *every step of your own sales process.*

In other words, show the same accountability VITO would.

VITO RULE #6 Be accountable for your own sales process.

Of course, you must *know* your process in order to take VITO-level responsibility for it. If it's your process, you must know what's going on within it. Period. There must be no cop-outs. No room for excuses. No room for rationalizations. You either know the process or you don't. You either execute the process or you don't.

Ideally, I would evaluate your sales process with you, step by step, in person so we could figure out together what you will be holding yourself accountable for. Since I don't know what your process looks like, I'll start by doing the next best thing, which is to give you a look at *my* sales process!

Here's how it breaks down:

Step 1: I send the VITO I want to sell to one of my best-selling books, along with a custom-made bookmark that outlines my value proposition for that VITO's company in one sentence. (By the way, the *only* VITOs I send this stuff to are those who fit my Template of Ideal Prospects; see Appendix A.)

I include a special letter I call a VITO letter, which you'll be learning a lot more about later on in this book. In that letter, I promise my target VITO a phone call at a specific date and time.

Step 2: I call at the appointed time to follow up.

> » No connection? I leave a powerful voice mail message. (You'll find out how to leave your own in Chapter 18.)
>
> » No return call? I leave another, slightly different, voice mail message—one each week for several weeks—until I receive a call back. (You'll learn how to vary your messages, too, also in Chapter 18.)

Step 3: I get a return call or make telephone connection with VITO. During that call, I find out if VITO's goals, plans, and objectives can be helped by my value proposition. If so, VITO and I move on quickly—*together*—to Step 4.

Step 4: I present the agreement; we sign it.

Step 5: I conduct the event.

Step 6: I track and broadcast results to all other divisions/sister companies; I generate referrals, both internal and external.

Step 7: Based upon the results, I suggest other products, services, and solutions that (you guessed it) add even greater value to my business relationship.

That's the process I'm accountable for executing. Now, I've already told you about the importance of time, so it will come as no surprise to you that I've got a clear sense of how long it takes me to move through all the steps of my process with a given company. The first five steps of this seven-step sales process can take anywhere from one to four months; the average is a little over two and a half months.

Right now, before you go any further in this book, write down each step of your own current sales process in the space that follows. Don't omit any steps, even if you sometimes skip them in an actual sale. *If you need to do it to generate revenue, list it.* Fill in as many of the blanks as you need to.

MY SALES PROCESS

Step 1 _____

Step 2 _____

Step 3 _____

Step 4 _____

Step 5 _____

Step 6 _____

Step 7 _____

Step 8 _____

Step 9 _____

Step 10 _____

Analyze Your Process

VITOs have a keen sense of what's essential and what's excess baggage in any process, including the sales process. You should, too.

Having reviewed thousands of sales processes over the years, I can attest that the quickest way to find out whether a given sales process is as effective and efficient as possible is to see what steps salespeople consistently ignore. For example, if the same three steps are being skipped over again and again by a given sales team, those steps are not needed to generate revenue. People who still invest time, effort, and energy in those steps are making bad investments.

Take a moment now to show your sales process to another salesperson on your team. Make sure this is someone you really respect, someone with a lot of experience and a clear record of current success selling for your company. *For now, steer clear of your manager* until you see how close you are to following the ideal sales process.

As you talk to your respected colleague, factor in the following questions:

First, are there any steps your colleague thinks you're missing?

Second, are there any steps you should be skipping? Specifically, are there any unnecessary elements of the process you're now being asked to perform for the sake of habit or internal "political" reasons, elements that don't actually generate revenue? For instance, are you being asked to get a physical copy of each prospect's most recent annual report, just so you can stuff it into a prospect folder? The most important numbers and words in an annual report can be obtained straight from the horse's mouth, while you're building effective business rapport with VITO. And these days, just about every annual report is available online! You can get access to all of them—quarterly, including interim manager's reports filed with the SEC—just by going to *www.edgar.org.*

Third, are there any steps that are typically ignored or blown off by your prospects? For instance: demos, presentations, proposals, loaner equipment, site visits.

Finally, are you being asked to fill in meaningless blanks . . . in obedience to your contact management system? For instance, is there a point in the formal sales process where your computer is demanding that you fill in a blank proving to your manager (or whoever) that you understand the needs of each level of buying influence? Some variation on this generic request has appeared in every formal sales process I've ever seen an organization come up with! In reality, that all-encompassing request for information can and should be distilled down to a few intelligent questions sprinkled throughout the entire sales process. It shouldn't be a single step at the beginning of the discussion, or anywhere else for that matter.

Go talk to a respected colleague right now. Then create a revised sales process on the following page.

Do this! Do not continue with the book until you understand, and are ready to assume full accountability for, your own sales process.

Remember—this is not your company's sales process. This is not your manager's sales process. It is *your* sales process.

MY *REVISED* SALES PROCESS, WHICH TAKES ADVANTAGE OF MY DISCUSSION WITH A SENIOR COLLEAGUE

Step 1 _____

Step 2 _____

Step 3 _____

Step 4 _____

Step 5 _____

Step 6 _____

Step 7 _____

Step 8 _____

Step 9 _____

Step 10 _____

Welcome Back—Now Have Some Fun!

For the next six prospects that you pursue, use your modified plan with the useless step(s) eliminated. See what happens. Don't tell your manager or anyone else what you're doing—they might "fire-hose" your plan. Does your new approach improve the:

» Elapsed time to obtain the first sale
» Ease of obtaining the first sale
» Number of steps you had to take to get the first sale
» Number of steps your prospect had to take to get the first sale approved
» Size of the first sale
» Number and amount of presales resources required to make the sale (in other words, does it reduce your company's, and your, front-end investment in the sale?)

Use the modified sales process you just created and track your results in the following areas:

1. Did you get the sale faster?
2. Did you use less presales resources?
3. Did you have fewer hassles with your own infrastructure?
4. Did you have more fun?

After you answer these questions, share your results with your sales manager and/or your Vice President of Sales. Why? Because you're a team player, that's why!

Improve the Process

You're not finished, of course. You will be improving this process, not just for the period of time when you are reading this book but for as long as you sell professionally.

VITOs have a responsibility to implement constant, never-ending improvement. This commitment requires them to look in every corner of their business for ideas to make whatever is being done be done better, faster, less expensive. You must make the same commitment.

Control Your Sales Process

VITOs are control freaks. You should be, too.

The secret to establishing control of your sales process is to *assume full accountability for it at all times.* Apply the following formula on a daily basis:

Control + Accountability = Greater Control

As you've already learned, your sales process is your responsibility, not anyone else's.

The essence of any process is that it is predictable and yields a certain result when followed. When any step of an effective proven process is forgotten or implemented too late, the result changes.

You want to fly where VITO flies? Good. Continue thinking like VITO thinks. VITO has a process for just about everything at VITO, Inc. If something goes wrong, VITO asks two critical questions:

1. What, if anything, did the process overlook?
2. What did I/you/we overlook in the process?

You must ask the same questions. Whenever a potential sale disappoints you, you must ask yourself those same two timeless questions.

VITO wouldn't rationalize, complain, or make excuses. Who has time for that? Follow VITO's lead. Eliminate the following thought paths from your mental floor plan:

» Why do these things always happen to me?
» It's the economy/marketplace/prospect that killed the deal.
» Our price was too high.
» The competition snagged the deal away from us at the bottom of the ninth.
» I/we lost the deal because of politics.

You know as well as I do that *all of these are cop-outs.* Don't invest your time, energy, or attention in them ever again.

Take a moment right now and write down, on a separate sheet of paper, the real reason(s) for the five worst sales disasters you've experienced. *What did the process overlook? What were you overlooking in the process?*

Be brutally honest with yourself—that's what VITO would do!

Chapter 4

Replicate, Replicate, Replicate

Replicate (v): to repeat, duplicate, or reproduce—*Dictionary.com*

VITO RULE #7

A process isn't a process unless you can replicate it.

Replication is the gold standard when it comes to selling to VITO. It's the culmination of all the work you've been doing in the past chapters and everything you will be learning in this and subsequent chapters. Success in sales, like success in any other field, is the result of preparation, hard work, and a process you can replicate.

Do you remember the Network of Influence and Authority I showed you in Chapter 1? Look at it again.

The Influence and Authority Network

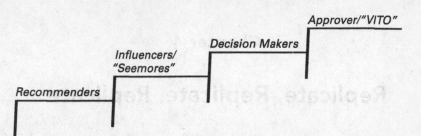

Of course, VITO sits at the very top of the organization. VITO has the ultimate veto power over absolutely everything that takes place in the organization. What I want to draw your attention to now, though, is not the eagle perched at the top of the pole but the resident of Linoleumville who sits close to the bottom of the organization. This person I call "Seemore."

Seemore can be male or female. Seemore has titles like Data Center Manager, Head IT Supervisor, Programmer, Research Analyst, Engineer, Buyer, Purchasing Agent, Head Accountant, Programmer—get the picture? Seemores are scientists, analysts, troubleshooters, and technical gurus. As good as they are at what they do, and as important as they are within the organization, they tend to drive us salespeople nuts! Why? Because they always want to *see more*. Hence the name: Seemore.

Seemore wants to see more presentations, more analysis, more data. Seemore wants more site visits, more demos, and more freebies. Seemore wants more boxes of donuts with the little sprinkly things on top. Whatever it is you can bring to the table, Seemore wants more of it. In fact, it's Seemores' job to get you to *bring* more of it to the table. I'd even go as far as to say that it's their mission in life.

What Seemore *doesn't* do (at least not without great difficulty) is make independent decisions at work, about purchases or anything else. In their capacity as subject-matter experts, Seemores' day-to-day job functions often include investigations of the different initiatives that need to take place in order to have successful outputs of whatever VITO, Inc. outputs. They find flaws. They identify trouble spots. They alert people who *do* make decisions to potential inconsistencies.

It's been my experience that Seemores are like hangers in a closet: they tend to multiply. You don't always know where they come from, but you know there are more of them this morning than there were yesterday. If you set up a meeting with one Seemore, when you show up for the meeting at the appointed time, you are likely to find *five* Seemores eagerly waiting to see you!

Whenever you read the word "Seemore" in this book, I want you to think of the person in the target organization who . . .

> *. . . Always . . .*

» Loves to discuss the details, functions, and feature set of what you sell

» Enjoys auditing and correcting the design of what you sell

» Has "better" ideas or improvements that could be made to what you sell

» Asks questions that require you to do some (or a lot of) research to answer

» Wants free stuff from you

» Tells you not to contact anyone else in the organization

» Tells you that he or she has the last word in the decision-making process (A side note: Have you ever noticed that VITOs rarely make this claim—even though it's absolutely true in their case? Seemores, on the other hand, make a habit of telling salespeople how important they are and how impossible it is for the project to move forward without their personal approval.)

. . . Only rarely . . .

» Returns your calls in a timely manner after the first interaction you have with him

» Has anything really good to say about what you sell

» Tells you what's really going on in his world

» Tells you how much money is in the budget

» Tells you who else he is looking at

» Introduces you to anyone else

. . . Never . . .

» Makes a decision on his or her own authority

Please keep all of these Seemore traits in mind as we move forward.

Do the VITO Dance

The most important part of the *upgraded and refined* sales process you will be building for yourself in this book is also the simplest to remember, and thus the simplest to replicate. It's called the VITO Dance. Doing the VITO Dance means taking the first steps in your sales process—outreach, initial voice mail and follow-up, and voice-to-voice contact—with VITO, rather than with Seemore (or anyone else). It's that simple.

Let me be clear here: I'm not saying you must eliminate Seemore from the sales process. If you forget all about Seemores, they will find a way to get even with you! They will sabotage anything and everything you try to sell. You *want* to keep Seemores involved. You *don't want* to begin your sales process with them.

The VITO dance is about putting VITO, intentionally and proactively, at the very front end of your sales process. No matter how you initiate that process in the first step, you will always put VITO first, whether you're sending a letter, post card, e-mail, leaving a voice-mail message, or kicking propaganda leaflets out of a low-flying ultralite that's buzzing VITO's parking lot.

When you reach out, *you will reach out to VITO first*. You will leave voice mail messages for VITO. You will make the initial voice-to-voice contact with either VITO or VITO's Personal Assistant. I will show you exactly how to do all that.

I can tell you from my own experience and the experience of over 2.5 million other salespeople that three very good things will happen when you hold yourself accountable for doing, and replicating, the VITO Dance.

1. You will get bigger initial sales—up to 54 percent bigger, as demonstrated by a major client of mine! Why would your initial sales size grow when you put VITO first? Because everything is bigger in VITO's world: the office, the desk, the responsibilities—some people might even say VITO's head is bigger! When VITO sees something he or she is personally convinced will help achieve any one of the big strategic initiatives in play between now and, let's say, the end of the fiscal year, VITO doesn't do a small play! VITO wants it everywhere it can possibly help. As a general but reliable rule, *when VITOs buy, they buy big.*

2. You will close deals faster—typically 50 percent faster! This, too, is only logical. VITOs are fast thinkers who take action quickly once they have examined all the angles. They are not going to wait around for anybody to do anything just for the sake of waiting. They're going to issue an order and buy whatever it is they want to buy. So, yes, you'll be selling stuff a whole lot sooner to VITO than you would if you were waiting

around for Seemore. So here's the story so far: You'll be landing bigger deals in less time, and that's going to yield fatter commission checks and over-quota performance sooner!

3. You will win more add-on business from your existing clients—up to 120 percent more, as my own client base has shown!

Do you remember the definition of a customer we agreed upon a little earlier? As in, "someone who actually pays money for your stuff in this calendar month"? Now that we've established that, I want you to think of your number-one customer. Got it? Excellent. Now, I want you to picture the VITO who runs that organization.

Have you ever *met* that VITO? Have you ever been in that VITO's office? If not, let me ask you this: Do you have all the business you deserve from that existing customer or just a thin slice? If you answered "thin slice," rejoice, because all of that is about to change . . . *if*.

THOSE THREE GOOD THINGS YOU JUST READ REALLY WILL HAPPEN TO YOU . . . *IF:*

You are willing to do the VITO Dance.

You are committed to holding yourself accountable for implementing your own sales process.

You are willing to fix what isn't currently working in your sales process and replace it with something that does work.

You completed all the written activities in Chapters 2 and 3. (Go do them right now if you zipped over them—they're important!)

You are willing to replicate your sales process.

You are willing to extend that sales process to your very best potential Advocates—the VITOs within your current accounts!

Why does VITO have Veto Power?

Jackie, a major account rep for one of the largest computer manufacturers in the world, had worked for seven months on a new opportunity she had uncovered during one of her prospecting blitzes. Potentially, it was a big deal; she and her support team had spent weeks performing studies, conducting analyses, giving demos, going on site visits, and making factory tours. She had finally gotten to the point where her solution was being sent "up the ladder" for approval. Her primary contact, the Chief Technology Officer (CTO), assured her that the review by the Board of Directors was just a formality, a "rubber stamp." After all, the board had approved the expense line for the project, and the CTO had been told in no uncertain terms by the CEO to "get it done." This was good news for Jackie, who was in position to make a sizable commission. Once she got past the "just a formality" phase, she was anticipating a check totaling just under $33,000—enough to put her in the top 10 percent of all salespeople for the year and win her an all-expenses-paid trip to Rome, courtesy of her employer, for making the Presidents' Club. Not bad! All was looking good for Jackie . . . until she got this ominous text message from the CTO: "Things are on hold." As it turned out, the CTO hadn't really done his homework—and Jackie hadn't done her sales work. The CEO had made a few calls to board members. He had used his veto power.

Ben sells human resource outsourcing services. He loves his job and his customers love him. He's not in the top tier of sellers for his company, but he has been making his quota for the past five years, and he's been a steady performer, which makes his sales manager happy. One day, a mid-sized company in his territory called him and asked for help in developing a proposal for a big project. "Wow," Ben thought, "all good things really do come to those who wait!" Off he ran to work with the VP of Human Resources. Four months and many lunch meetings later, his sales forecast showed one of the largest opportunities in his district, estimated at a solid 95 percent probability to close. He had been spending a lot of time on this deal, and had told his manager he expected it to close during the last month of the last quarter of the fiscal year. All eyes were on Ben—and on his opportunity. The company needed this deal to close the year in the black, and Ben needed this deal to make his quarter for the year! He had stopped doing a lot of his normal prospecting, and he didn't have any other deals to speak of in his pipeline. Unfortunately, the weekend before the end of the quarter, Ben got word from his contact that the president of the company he was trying to sell to had decided to change his company's priorities. He had used his veto power to kill the deal. Ben's company finished the year in the red—and so did Ben.

These stories are based on real events. These kinds of disasters happen on a daily basis, but *why* do they happen?

Guess What?

Your "decision maker" isn't really the decision maker.

VITO RULE #8	Above every Decision Maker, and above every decision in the enterprise, sits VITO— the approver of the sale and everything else.

Have *you* ever worked on a deal for a long time, jumped through all the hoops, and then, after having been told by your contact that you had the business, lost it?

Sure you have! What happened? VITO stepped in and exercised veto power, that's what happened!

Let's look again at Jackie's situation. She didn't have all the information she needed. Specifically, she didn't know that VITO and three of the board members are major stock holders in one of Jackie's biggest competitors. *All of her work—every single minute of it—was in vain.* She never had a shot at that deal. If she'd connected with VITO first, she would have figured that out in less than five minutes.

In Ben's end-of-the-year nightmare, something very similar happened. The CEO happened to have a fishing buddy whose company was bought up by an outsourcing company. That outsourcing company could do what the CEO wanted done, so he went with them. In this case, Ben didn't know that the competitor had entered the game until it was too late. Ben was not in VITO's loop.

For Jackie and Ben, the result and lesson was the same. They both lost, and they both learned that VITO, the Very Important Top Officer, has the ultimate veto power.

What's Your Story?

Over the years, I've had a lot of people try to tell me about exceptions to the VITO Rule I've just shared with you. They say things like . . .

> » This VITO is only a figurehead.
> » This VITO doesn't get involved in these kinds of decisions.
> » We tried something like this before, and all it did was irritate my current contact.

Let me be frank with you: These are all rationalizations, dodges, justifications, excuses for *doing things the way you are used to doing them*. If you keep doing things the way you have always done them, you will keep getting the results you have always gotten. Specifically, you will *keep investing time, effort, and resources in deals that drop off the radar screen once VITO exercises the right to veto.* If that's happened to you even once, and I bet it has, my question for you now is a simple one: *How much did that cost you?*

Forget the rationalizations. Forget the excuses. Forget about what you're used to doing. When you get right down to it, the only reality that matters is this: There is one and only one person who has the ultimate influence, authority, and veto power over everyone and everything in the enterprise, including your sale, and that person is VITO.

I realize you may believe that VITO is too intimidating to approach. VITO has the biggest set of responsibilities. VITO typically pulls the largest paycheck, has the biggest comp plan, the fattest benefits, and the most perks. As if all of that weren't enough, VITO typically has the biggest ego of anyone in the organization. *These are the real reasons people don't want to reach out to VITO!*

Regardless, you need VITO on your side—period. That means you need to reach out to VITO first. If you're still uncertain about whether you can commit to this, keep reading. In the next chapter, I'll share the six big reasons why contacting VITO's office first is an absolute must-have in your sales process.

Chapter 5

Six Big Reasons to Contact VITO First

Whether we *like* it or not . . . whether we want to *admit* it or not . . . whether we choose to *do* anything about it or not . . . VITO always has the veto power over whether our stuff actually gets bought or gets kicked out the door.

VITO RULE #9

No matter what anyone else in the buying enterprise has to say about some salesperson's offering, VITO can (and often will) kill that offering on a moment's notice.

This is a fact of sales life. You are better off accepting it, and adapting to it, sooner than later. If you feel any hesitation about updating your sales process so it reflects this core selling reality, you should consider these six indisputable reasons why VITO really does equal veto in your world, and why you *must* contact VITO first.

1. VITO Creates Every Important Initiative

By definition, an important initiative at VITO, Inc. only *becomes* important when VITO buys into it. Every critical goal, plan, and objective at VITO, Inc. has VITO's DNA in it. Others in the organization can feed the suggestion box, but VITO decides what's hot and what's not at any given moment. As we have seen, VITO's mind can change on a dime and may do so without VITO asking anybody anything.

If you want to stay in the know about what's really important at any given moment at VITO, Inc., keep your hand on VITO's pulse and put VITO's private telephone number on speed dial throughout your entire relationship with the company.

2. Constant Improvement is VITO's Responsibility

In VITO's world, status quo doesn't go. VITOs are measured on the growth of their organizations. Flat, horizontal growth lines just don't compute for VITO, stakeholders, and shareholders; therefore, they're on a constant lookout for ideas that no one else has brought to their attention. They have an "early adopter" mentality; they are eager to take the risk to have what no one else has and do what no one else is doing.

In other words, they are likely to be the most receptive people in the entire organization to well-designed sales offerings that actually add value to VITO, Inc.

True Story

Several years ago, I offered my services to the third largest telecommunications company in the world. I had never done business in the telecom industry! I had no proof that my stuff would work for them, but what I did have was a strong *suspicion* that, because of my experience in other industries, I could deliver something similar or even greater for this major carrier. In a very short time, I put together a deal that gave them exclusive rights to me within the telecom industry for two years. How did I do it? *By calling VITO first.* I was able to articulate my "suspected value" in a way that proved to VITO that I had something that would give that huge telecom company the edge. I didn't have any experience within that industry: What I did have was a well-founded suspicion and the willingness to call VITO directly. Pretty soon, VITO had a hunch that my hunch could pay off for his company. Both of our hunches paid off!

3. VITO Owns all Budgets

When your current contact says, "We've got to get the budget approved," who do you think that person goes to for approval? Answer: Either to VITO or to someone who reports, directly or indirectly, to VITO. Depending upon how low on the company totem pole the person is that you're dealing with, the budget request may have several levels to travel, but the stream always flows in the same direction. *Notice this*: Every other person in the organization is told how much they can spend, and tries to spend less than they have so they can look like a hero in VITO's eyes. That's why you're always being asked by these underlings to lower your price. VITO, on the other hand, *has* no budget. Or, if you prefer, VITO can say, at any given moment, "Let there be a budget for X," and suddenly, there's a budget!

If you want to eliminate the price objection from your life (and who doesn't), I can show you exactly how. Contact VITO first. Then, during your very first interaction with VITO, state your price clearly and confidently. (I like to pull out my standard agreement and let VITO look it over on the spot.) If there is haggling to be done, you and VITO will do it here, and you'll get it over with before you invest massive amounts of time and energy in the deal. More often than you might expect, you'll name your price and VITO will nod and ask what else there is to talk about. Once VITO decides to work with you, VITO will allocate sufficient funds to the appropriate decision maker.

4. VITO Knows Who's Who

VITO not only *knows* everyone of importance on the org chart, but also (most likely) hand-picked, hired, or held on to everyone on that chart. VITO typically has less than ten direct reports. These individuals are VITO's movers and shakers, the people who get done whatever VITO wants done. Investing large amounts of your time with anyone else in the enterprise amounts to sales malpractice.

5. VITO Defines the Critical Business Criteria

At VITO, Inc., there are certain critical business criteria that all partners and suppliers must meet or exceed if they want to exchange their goods for VITO's cold, hard cash. Can you guess who sets those criteria? I thought you could. Some of these criteria are "hard" measurables expressed in numbers and percentages and take the form of revenue increases, reliability ratings, performance history, projected savings, and so on. Some of these criteria are "soft" values articulated with descriptive words and phrases such as "brand reputation," "compliance," "internal morale," "goodwill," "prestige among VITO's peers," and so on.

If you and your company can't meet VITO's business criteria, you will be dismissed. If you don't know what the criteria are, you can't meet them.

6. VITO Gets Paid to Make Decisions

This one's a no-brainer. You're a salesperson. Your job is to generate positive decisions from qualified people who have the authority to say yes to mutually beneficial business propositions. VITO's job is to make decisions that benefit VITO, Inc. This is a match made in heaven!

Some others in the enterprise avoid making decisions, but VITO knows that making a decision is the only sure way to get the ball rolling. VITOs love to get the ball rolling . . . and keep it rolling! So, as the classic film *Ghostbusters* asked: Who you gonna call? Someone who hates making decisions? Or someone who makes decisions for a living?

What's driving those decisions? The nine values that drive VITO's decisions are as follows:

1. *Competence*. VITO's decision-making actions will typically be based upon experience, reason, and moral principles. There's an emotional component, too, but VITO is too smart a player not to look at the upsides and downsides.

2. *Forward-looking vision*. VITOs set clear goals and envision the future, then make decisions that match that vision. They know where they're going. They habitually pick priorities that support their vision.

3. *Confidence*. VITOs displays confidence in all that they do, especially when it comes to making a decision.

49

4. *Intelligence.* VITOs quickly get access to the background information they need. They are well informed and well connected, and as a result they tend to make good decisions fast.

5. *Fair-mindedness.* VITOs are open-minded and fair. Contrary to popular belief, they are generally sensitive to the feelings, values, interests, and well being of others.

6. *Broad-mindedness.* VITOs instinctively seek out diversity, and in doing so, open up their world of possibilities.

7. *Honesty.* VITOs are straight shooters. They will always tell you where you stand.

8. *Imagination.* VITOs know how to make timely and appropriate changes in their thinking, plans, and methods. They are always on the lookout for new and better ideas and solutions to problems.

9. *Courage.* VITOs don't spook easily, and they have the perseverance to accomplish a goal, regardless of the seemingly insurmountable obstacles they may face. Specifically, they are not frightened of making the "wrong" decision. When this happens, VITOs simply make another decision and move on!

Close-Up on the Decision Maker

Effective VITO selling does not rule out the involvement of other players at VITO, Inc. To the contrary: Knowing how to approach and interact with all other players is critical to a successful VITO launch. In this section, you will begin the ongoing, career-long mission of developing an in-depth understanding of the traits, likes, dislikes, and potential business relationship pitfalls you will encounter when dealing with three people. All three work at VITO, Inc.; all three are likely to show up at some point in your sales process.

They are:

1. **The Decision Maker.** This is VITO's direct report.
2. **"Seemore," the Influencer.** This is a technical/topic expert who typically does not report directly to VITO, but who can derail your sale if you're not careful.
3. **The Recommender.** This is an end-user or potential end-user of your stuff who typically does not report directly to VITO.

Let's look now at the members of the most important group on that list: the Decision Makers who are personally accountable to VITO for *overachieving* on VITO's vision.

The Decision Maker

I have yet to meet a VITO who didn't handpick his or her own direct reports; that is, someone who answers *personally* to VITO, week in and week out. This elite group ranges from Personal Assistants to the individuals who run the divisions and lines of business that drive VITO, Inc. These hand picked, highly accountable folks are loyal not just to VITO but to VITO's vision. They make up an inner circle at VITO, Inc. Always remember, that inner circle *includes* VITO's Personal Assistant.

These people take it as their job description to make happen whatever VITO wants to happen—sooner rather than later.

For the most part, this elite group of *direct reports* can be gathered into the category I call Decision Makers. They are compensated (quite handsomely, I might add) for the *overaccomplishment* of VITO's vision and mission. They want to raise the bar, which is why VITO likes having them around.

Decision Makers typically have titles like Line of Business Executive, Director, VP, or CXO. That "X" could stand for just about anything: Financial, Technology, Information, Operations, Marketing, Sales, Performance, Learning, and so on. But don't get too distracted by job titles; occasionally, a Personal Assistant who has been handpicked by VITO and who puts in years of loyal service rises to the level of Decision Maker in all but name.

Good relationships with Decision Makers are critical to your ability to make the sale at VITO, Inc. and to your overall success within the enterprise.

For the most part, Decision Makers are upwardly mobile, highly visible types. They are politically astute, and they love to broadcast positive news about themselves and their area of responsibility. They are good self-promoters, and, as a general rule, they are fearless. They know the operational terrain at VITO, Inc. well, and they know how to navigate the political currents. Any company has its challenges; whenever a big storm hits at VITO, Inc, you'll usually find that VITO and the Decision Makers are the first ones who have landed on their feet.

Decision Makers live to:

> » Add massive value by fulfilling the organizational vision
> » Get credit and rewards for doing so

These are sought-after players, and it's not uncommon for them to move from one company to another in search of greater challenges and greater rewards. Once you earn their trust, they will take you with them wherever they go. This is one huge reason why we must follow the Decision Maker's example. Just as the Decision Maker *overfulfills* on every promise made to VITO, we must *overfulfill* on every promise we make to a Decision Maker.

A True Story

Bill was the VP of Sales at YadaYada Company when I met him. That was twelve years ago. When I got an e-mail from him recently, a big smile came across my face! My relationship with Bill and his team at YadaYada had been a very successful one . . . so successful, in fact, that he wanted my help in his new capacity as Senior VP of Sales at Whatchamacallit Unlimited. The text of Bill's e-mail was music to my ears: "Tony, I want you to help my new sales force do what you did at YadaYada." Talk about a one-call close! This one was a one e-mail close. When Bill and I connected by phone, I asked him: *"If you and I could redo what we accomplished at YadaYada, what, if anything, would you do differently?"* Keep that one in your pocket, and when a Decision Maker that you've worked with in the past calls you, lay that one on them!

Decision Makers are basically "yes" people. That doesn't mean they're incapable of thinking for themselves, but it does mean that when they are given a set of goals, plans, and objectives from VITO, they *must* fulfill. Sure, they can give VITO supportive opinions and information that illustrate options and alternate ways to overaccomplish the task. What they can't do, though, is push back with responses like: *"This is impossible." "Where do you expect me to get the resources to do this?" "This is more of the same nonsense as last year . . . when will we ever learn?"* Other people in the organization may be able to get away with that kind of talk, but not Decision Makers. Instead, you will hear Decision Makers saying things like:

> » This looks great.
> » My team can do it.
> » Let's get started.

Picture a meeting between VITO and Jackie, who is the Chief Operations Officer at VITO, Inc. Here's what VITO says:

"Jackie, I want you to find the fastest way to get our production increased by 15 percent between now and the end of this quarter. When you report back to me tomorrow, give me all the risks and costs involved with that. And don't forget to take into consideration the union labor restrictions."

If Jackie were then to say:

"Mr. VITO, that target and timeframe are completely unrealistic. This kind of thing has been tried before. I'm afraid it simply can't be done."

Jackie would be one click closer to surfing job sites. In effect, she would be saying, "VITO, please take me out of the inner circle."

Now you see what I mean when I say that VITO's Decision Makers are "yes" people. They've *got* to say yes. They get paid to say yes . . . to VITO, and to the principle of getting the job done.

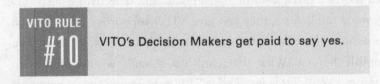

VITO RULE #10 VITO's Decision Makers get paid to say yes.

You can relate to this, can't you? Would you look your sales manager in the eye and say, "No, I can't prospect for new business"? Or "No, I'm not going to update my sales forecast"? Or "No, I can't set up that meeting"?

Just like you, the Decision Maker must salute and say, "Yes." Here's the beautiful part: Whenever that happens, the Decision Maker goes into "acquisition" mode. As in, "How in the world do I acquire an asset, resource, or ally that will overaccomplish this seemingly impossible goal for VITO?" Of course, we want the Decision Maker to do that "acquiring" from us!

Six Rules of Engagement for the Decision Makers VITO Points You Toward

To make that "acquiring" happen as quickly and profitably as possible for both sides, you must *get VITO to point you toward* a specific Decision Maker. (You'll learn all about how to do that in future chapters.) Once you've won that golden referral, you must follow these Six Rules of Engagement for Dealing with Decision Makers.

1. Celebrate, respect, listen to, and act upon the opinions, perceptions, or advice of any Decision Maker VITO refers you to. Remember, these people are empowered by VITO with significant influence and authority within the organization.

2. Focus on tactical issues, not strategic initiatives, whenever you ask the Decision Maker questions.

3. Let the Decision Maker do most of the talking. And while he or she is talking, listen carefully and take notes. Decision Makers tend to build alliances with people who have good listening skills.

4. Focus on exchanges that involve reactions, feelings, and responses. Find out how the Decision Maker feels about the job he or she has been given by VITO.

5. Make brief, credible, and sincere compliments. Stature and acknowledgment are extremely important to these folks.

6. Keep your conversations uncluttered and free of too many details. Stay at the 30,000-foot level and focus on "thumbnail sketches" of the *advantages* of what your product, service, and solutions could possibly do for their specific line of business and/or area of responsibility. Stay away from the minutia, techno-babble, and industry jargon. If you ask the Decision Maker a question about something he or she doesn't know or

care about (or, even worse, start to lecture the Decision Maker about such a topic), you will be *wasting your precious referral from VITO* by issuing a direct challenge to the Decision Maker's power, control, and authority—and that's not cool! If you ever make this mistake, you will immediately be shunted to Seemore, who is the *Decision Maker's* direct report. You'll learn more on how to deal with Seemore in the next chapter.

AN IMPORTANT NOTE ON ADVANTAGES

When I say that your discussions with the Decision Maker should focus on *advantages*, here's what I mean: **An advantage** is how you tailor, tweak, modify, customize, and implement whatever you sell to make it relevant and fit perfectly with your prospects'/ customers' needs. An advantage is *not* what your product "is" or how it "does" whatever it's been designed to do. It is, rather, what you will do to ensure that your prospect or customer gets the jump on a) the competition, b) VITO, Inc.'s current way of doing whatever it is doing, or c) both a and b as a direct result of using your stuff.

Chapter 6

Influencers and Recommenders

Decision Makers are busy folks. They have lots of meetings to attend, customers and suppliers to entertain, reports to pore over, conference calls to participate in. They can't do it all on their own, so they gather a group of individuals to do the heavy lifting for them.

I call the technical experts who help Decision Makers "Seemores." Their job is to see more and provide *more*: more data, more research, more facts, and more figures—all for the purpose of influencing the Decision Maker. The main thing to remember about Seemore is that he or she does not, can not, and has no authority to take any action remotely resembling a decision.

Why not? Because that's the Decision Maker's job!

Now, if you equate making a decision to buying (and if you've been selling for more than about a week, I'm sure you do), then, by logical deduction, you must come to embrace the following self-evident VITO rule:

> **VITO RULE #11**
> Influencers can't buy jack. Never could. Never would. Never will. Period. End of story.

Therefore, if you find yourself in the unhealthy position of trying to sell anything to an Influencer, you should bear in mind that, by continuing down this path, you will get the same result you would if you were trying to teach a pig to sing. You might irritate the pig, but you will never, ever, get to the desired outcome, no matter what.

Although there may well be times when you'll have to interact with Seemore (who can, as I have pointed out, kill your sale), the fact remains that you must NOT get pigeonholed with Seemore (spend all of your time with Seemore without gaining any visibility into the movement, or lack thereof, of your sales process with the Decision Maker and VITO). Instead, you must follow what I call The Six Rules of Engagement with Influencers.

Seemore Rule Number One

Never ask Seemore: *"Who besides yourself will be making this decision?"*

Seemore Rule Number Two

Never ask Seemore any variation on: *"What would you like to see next?"* or *"What would you like for me to do next?"*

Seemore Rule Number Three

When you don't know the answer to a question that Seemore asks, *don't* guess, make stuff up, or wing it or take a SWAG (Stupid Wild-Ass Guess) at answering it.

Seemore Rule Number Four

Whenever you make a promise to get something for Seemore, make sure you get it into Seemore's hands *exactly* when you say you're going to, and not a second earlier or later.

Seemore Rule Number Five

Always remember that Seemore's opinion is taken into careful consideration by the Decision Maker(s). Translation: Don't burn bridges with this person.

Seemore Rule Number Six

By the same token, you should remember that Seemore's opinions are not the final word on anything. Like any other "opinion," they may be acknowledged and taken or ignored by the Decision Maker(s).

The first four rules of engagement are obvious and really don't require any additional words of wisdom from me. However, I do want to go into a little more depth on rules five and six.

The Decision Makers of the world really do trust and rely upon Seemore to give them an accurate take on all of the possible options open for them to get the job done. There is typically more than one right answer to any problem, and this is where the challenge lies for us as professional salespeople.

Consider the following typical scenario: The Decision Maker is given a goal by VITO. Let's say it's, "Find a lower cost supplier for new ATM machines that can support the South American market, with full deployment by year's end."

What happens next?

The Decision Maker tells Seemore to find at least *three* ways to accomplish the goal by the end of the *second quarter* (note: that's early) and to make sure that the supplier can cut 15 percent off the purchase price. (Note again: Decision Makers love to pad their requests to Seemore; VITO didn't request the 15 percent cut.)

Now Seemore heads off to "lock in" three suppliers, pitting one against the other, and upping the ante along the way. Seemore is now looking for deep discounts of up to *20 percent* from a global supplier of ATMs with capabilities in South America!

Just remember this: The further away you get from VITO, the more "interpretation" you get about what is really needed at VITO, Inc. And notice the quote marks around the word "interpretation."

Recommenders: Meet Seemore's Splinter Group

The old saying holds that there's strength in numbers, and Seemore, the Influencer, would certainly agree with that.

Influencers love to make sure that whatever they've been asked to present to a Decision Maker is correct. They want everything tested to the highest degree, and they want all the facts and figures worked out to the seventeenth decimal place. That's a lot for one person to provide. Even someone as capable as Seemore!

It's typical for Influencers who are out to test, evaluate, prove, disprove, or otherwise triple- and quadruple-check something to recruit a faction of individuals from other parts of the organization and ask for their input/opinions. These recruits may come from areas such as administration, manufacturing, procurement, sales, marketing, engineering, facilities, management, and, yes, even the janitorial staff. Anyone who can provide additional information, particularly "soft" data that typically cannot be calculated or quantified, may be asked to pitch in. Potential end-users of a given product or service are particularly likely to be asked to serve as recruits.

We call the people Seemore asks for help in assembling a body of data to show to the Decision Maker by a special name: Recommenders. They usually don't form a separate unit, work group, or department at VITO, Inc. Think of them as an ad hoc splinter group convened by Seemore for the purpose of:

» Testing a procedure that Seemore is evaluating
» Certifying a critical component that needs to be evaluated for durability
» Giving feedback on a process at VITO, Inc. that's being considered for modification
» And so on

Anything that needs confirmation can be bestowed upon this group of people by Seemore, the Influencer. After a certain "incubation" time, Seemore will expect a comprehensive study or report from this group, one that culminates in a formal *recommendation* that Seemore can pass along to the Decision Maker as substantiating evidence. Notice that Seemore virtually never makes an independent recommendation; Seemores are much more comfortable passing along data and recommendations that come from other people: Recommenders.

Here are the Six Rules of Engagement for dealing with Recommenders.

Recommender Engagement Rule Number One
Never ask a Recommender to make a decision or take sides.

Recommender Engagement Rule Number Two
Never ask a Recommender to give you any information that may be considered private, or that Seemore is not willing to give to you.

Recommender Engagement Rule Number Three
Never give the Recommender any information that you don't want shared with all of VITO, Inc. If you say, "Don't tell this to anyone, but . . ." it is very likely the Recommender will translate what you have just said as, "Please share the following information with everyone you see hanging out near the water cooler tomorrow morning."

Recommender Engagement Rule Number Four

Be sure to ask a Recommender, in private if possible, about his or her personal experience and/or insights with issues relating to your product, service, or solution or what they're currently using. See what comes back.

Recommender Engagement Rule Number Five

You can ask the Recommender for advice *if and only if* you know you are not asking him or her to break any rules by passing along that advice.

Recommender Engagement Rule Number Six

If you wish, you may find a way to thank Recommenders in a special way, as long your gratitude could not possibly be perceived as a professional bribe.

Now That You Know It All . . .

Think carefully about how *your* sales process should anticipate and strategize contacts with people in the four levels I've outlined: VITO, the Decision Maker, Seemore the Influencer, and the Recommender.

In case you're looking for advice on this question here's what I suggest. Make your first call on VITO the Approver.

» Cover three very important first-call objectives during that call (you'll be learning exactly how to do that in the chapters that follow).
» Qualify this business opportunity (ditto).
» Then, take the shunt to the Decision Maker (you'll be learning exactly how to facilitate this in the chapters that follow).

» Then, before you make contact with the Decision Maker, gather some information from either the resources on the web or from a Recommender or two.

» After you build Equal Business Stature with the Decision Maker and position yourself from a business criteria standpoint (you'll be learning how to do that too!) . . .

» *Then and only then,* you'll spend time with Seemore and start building your coalition.

Throughout this process (which is, by the way, the perfect sales process, capable of getting you to the top of your game faster than a speeding bullet, locomotive, or high-speed connection to the Internet), you will, I repeat, *will,* follow each and every one of the rules of engagement that I have shared with you!

VITO RULE

#12 Follow the perfect sales process.

Are we cool with all that? I thought so. Let's move on to the next chapter.

Chapter 7

How Not to Communicate
with VITO

Lots of salespeople get this far in the program and think, *"This all sounds great, Tony, but I still have one burning question: What, exactly, do you want me to say to VITO?"*

These good folks know that selling to VITO is a contact sport, and they know that I'm eventually going to ask them to reach out to VITO. They've heard about how the *Selling to VITO* system emphasizes direct, voice-to-voice, person-to-person contact with VITO. And by the time they reach this part of the VITO course, they're looking for one thing and one thing only: a script.

In other words, they are willing to consider using the system I'm outlining for them in this book . . . if. If I promise give them a sheet of paper with the magic words written on it that will turn VITO into a calm, compliant pussycat on the phone.

You should know right now: No such sheet exists, should exist, or can exist!

There is no magic script. There are some broad *guidelines* for having a great call with VITO—and I'll cover them in detail with you— but there's no single speech you can memorize ahead of time and then recite verbatim to get appointments.

VITO RULE #13 Like VITO, you have to be willing to change course as circumstances demand in order to hit your goal.

I want to be up-front with you about this early on, so that by the time we *do* get to the part where you pick up the phone and call the corner office on the top floor at VITO, Inc., you're ready for what's really going to be happening and you've got the right expectations in place about what has to happen *before* that call.

Something Better Than a Script

The voice-to-voice contact with VITO (which is what most salespeople I work with are scared of) is only *part* of the equation. It's an important part, to be sure, but not, by any means, the whole toolkit. That's because we're going to be communicating with VITO in many ways, not just by phone. Because we're going to be reaching out to VITO persistently via multiple media, and because most of the salespeople we'll be competing with either don't reach out to VITO at all or make basic mistakes with VITO that sabotage their conversations within seconds, I want to share something even better than a script with you in this chapter.

I want you to memorize the following list of three classic mistakes. These are the major blunders salespeople usually make when reaching out to VITO, and they apply to verbal, written, and face-to-face communication.

Think of what follows as a short course in *how not to communicate with VITO*. Forget about the script you may want to memorize. Memorize this instead!

Committing any one of the following errors is likely to result in:

1. *A breakdown in communication.* VITO stops returning calls, cancels scheduled meetings, or takes his or her sweet time in responding to requests (as in never).
2. *A breach in building business rapport.* This means bringing up objections that are insurmountable and unanswerable late in the sales cycle . . . or maybe even not bringing them up at all.
3. *A loss or breaking of trust.* This means doubting what the salesperson has presented and or promised, suspected, or predicted.
4. *A loss of the sale.* This means you think you are doing much better than you actually are, and you get blindsided by the loss of the opportunity in the bottom of the ninth inning.

To avoid any of those nasty outcomes, you will take a solemn vow, here and now, to avoid *all* of the following mistakes in *all* of the communications you will initiate with VITO.

Mistake 1: Not Focusing on Benefits

Focusing on benefits means speaking what I call the "language of VITO." A *benefit* is an anticipated end result that brings VITO measurably closer to attaining some specific part of his or her vision. The moment you stop communicating about benefits, *you will lose VITO.*

Will what you're offering increase the shareholder value at VITO, Inc. by one or more of the following familiar results?

» Make VITO money
» Improve efficiency
» Save VITO money
» Keep VITO in compliance

Connect what you want to say to those benefits! When you stop to think about it, you will realize why it's so important to speak this kind of language. VITO has to deal with a lot of challenges on the average day: obstacles to the growth of VITO, Inc., labor issues, compliance, mergers and acquisitions, market challenges, and fiscal responsibilities, to name just a few. You want to focus, first and foremost, on the *benefit(s)* of your products, service, and solutions, and how they will help VITO overachieve goals, plans, and objectives for the near term and in the long range in all areas of VITO, Inc.

Salesperson on the phone to VITO: Mr. Importanta, the new insurance plan we're offering incorporates a user-friendly interface that will enable your employees at VITO, Inc. to more easily access their information.

VITO: (Click)

There are four different constituencies at VITO, Inc., and each speaks a very different language. (See the box below.) The number-one mistake salespeople make when communicating with VITO is not speaking the language of VITO!

COMMUNICATING WITH THE PLAYERS AT VITO, INC.

When communicating with **VITO**, focus on measurable *benefits* (end result that will match VITO's goals, plans, and objectives) during a particular period of time.

When communicating with the **Decision Maker**, focus on *advantages* (what you will do to tweak, modify, customize, or implement what you sell; how what you sell will provide an edge over the competition, and/or what's currently being used or the status quo at VITO, Inc.).

When communicating with **Seemore** the Influencer, focus on *features* (the pieces, parts, and components that make up what your product, service, and solution actually is).

When communicating with the **Recommender,** focus on *functions* (how people will actually use your product, service, and solution; the stuff you would put in an owner's manual).

Mistake 2: Using Terminology That VITO Doesn't Understand

This is a direct challenge to VITO's ego, power, control, influence, and authority. Always introduce your ideas, thoughts, and proposed solutions using words and phrases that VITO is familiar with and will accept.

Salesperson on the phone to VITO: Ms. Importanta, it looks like our new Cripton generator with its 28mx virtualized software application equalizer will perform with your existing NAP applications while giving you full security against any breach of your relational XT-data base.

VITO: Hold on, my assistant will help you. I've got more important compliance issues to deal with.

Wrong hymn book! The salesperson was pitching a feature to someone who couldn't care less about features, using techno-babble and terminology that only Seemore could understand!

Mistake 3: Not Respecting VITO's Time

VITOs live to overaccomplish their goals, plans, and objectives *ahead of schedule*. They divide the world up into two groups: those who keep them from beating the clock and those who help them beat the clock. Which camp would you rather be assigned to?

Salesperson on the phone to VITO: What I'd like to do is set up an in-person meeting with all of my team members so we can give you a full briefing.

VITO: (Click)

Believe it or not, VITO isn't looking forward to a full briefing from a group of total strangers. VITO lives in a time-compressed world— and if you stop to think about it, you'll realize that you do, too.

Take another look at those three big mistakes, and memorize them, before you go on to the next chapter!

Not focusing on benefits

Using terminology that VITO doesn't understand

Not respecting VITO's time

Here's my promise to you: Memorizing these three mistakes—and avoiding them—will get you a lot further than memorizing any script ever would!

Chapter 8

Twelve Attitudes and Traits You Must Own to Sell to VITO

When it comes to success in sales, the name of the game is SELLING TO VITO, and the very first thing you will be selling is your own Equal Business Stature.

You should know right now that everything you will be implementing from this point forward in the book is predicated on the idea that you and VITO are *functional equals*. I am not talking about titles or salary or perks or country club memberships or zip codes or stock portfolio values. I am taking about your *right* to interact with VITO one on one. I am talking about your attitudes, traits, and behaviors. I am talking about your willingness to *fly like an eagle*—just like VITO does—and run your world from the topmost perch—just like VITO does.

You must maintain *Equal Business Stature* in all your interactions with VITO, whether they are verbal, written, virtual, or sent up via smoke signals from a distant mountain. You have a right to initiate this relationship. You have a right to support it. You have a right to document the value you have delivered within it.

You have a right (and an obligation) to channel your own inner VITO, by means of twelve specific traits/attitudes. In this chapter, I outline all twelve.

71

What I am about to share with you is the culmination of my practical, one-on-one observations of VITOs over three decades. This is how they operate on a day-to-day basis. This is how they look at the world. This is how they post results. *After each element, I have left you a clear, simple question:* **Do I own this trait or will I own it by the time I finish this book?** When you can answer "Yes" to all twelve, you will know that you are ready not just to learn but to implement the tactics that follow in this book.

When you own all twelve of these traits, establishing and maintaining Equal Business Stature with VITO will be second nature to you. Remember: If title to title counted for anything in sales, not much of anything would ever be sold.

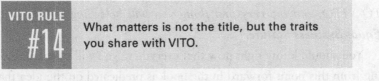

VITO RULE #14 — What matters is not the title, but the traits you share with VITO.

Okay, let's get started!

1. I Am Passionate About Life and Business

VITOs enjoy a high emotional state without the use of any substance, stimulant, or exotic New Age "therapies" or "activities." When VITOs get up in the morning, they picture the world of abundance that awaits, and they're excited about the opportunity that this day gives them: 1,440 minutes that, when gone, are gone forever. They seize the day with excitement. VITOs are not wishy-washy, indifferent, or doubtful. Their passion touches everything they do, both in their personal life and their business operations. They are grateful for each day.

I currently own this trait, or will own it by the time I finish this book. (Yes/No)

2. I Have Established a Good Work/Life Balance

VITOs know that all work and no play is a train wreck waiting to happen. Sure, it takes a lot of work to be successful in any economy, any market, with any product, service, or solution. However, VITOs know they must recharge their batteries. They know how to pace themselves, and they know what gives them rest and pleasure. They are engaged in activities outside of work that provide them with another venue for their interests and aptitudes. When you take a close look at the most successful and happiest VITOs (or anyone else for that matter), you will always find that individual to be engaged, in a balanced way, in both work and in life. The secret, VITOs know, is to put their work inside their life and not to put their life inside their work.

I currently own this trait, or will own it by the time I finish this book. (Yes/No)

3. I Am Constantly Expanding My Communication Skills

Are you committed to constantly perfecting your auditory, visual, and kinesthetic communications skills? (I'll wait here if you need to look those words up . . . okay, welcome back.) Typically, when VITO communicates, you get not just facts, but emotion in their message. They are usually good orators, and most of them can get the point across with pen and paper. When they speak, others listen, and they often speak using "word pictures," in other words they paint pictures that are easy for the listener(s) to see. Sure, some have speech writers and some use teleprompters, but most VITOs that you and I will work with are "do it yourselfers." They are good at engaging people, and their message is infectious. It's hard not to catch the wave when a VITO does the talking. Because they're constantly expanding their communication skills, their posture, vocabulary, diction, style, and ideas are appealing to a wide variety of individuals.

I currently own this trait, or will own it by the time I finish this book. (Yes/No)

4. I Am Curious

If you have children or you've spent time around them, you know that they are curious. For a successful VITO, it's all about being curious in a meaningful (and yes, occasionally childlike) way. For example, you'll notice that VITOs will ask questions that others may think of but are too insecure to ask. Recently, while in a meeting with VITO— president of a large, three-initial organization—I was explaining my Broadcast Center and how it can deliver "passive" revenue. Several questions came up about the tracking, market price, value, and deliverables from the other "C" level executives in the room. During that Q&A, VITO remained quite for a while and then asked, "Where did you get the idea that led to the development of this?" That one question changed the direction of the balance of the meeting, as we explored the commonalties of my vision and VITO's vision, and where VITO, Inc. was heading. What we discovered was a common interest we (VITO and I) had in the way we see our futures and how we manifest ideas. What's interesting to note is that this VITO has more than 6,000 employees; I have four. Curiosity has no limits, but it sure creates ideas that bond individuals and organizations together.

I currently own this trait, or will own it by the time I finish this book. (Yes/No)

5. I Am Self-Determined

VITOs believe it's their own responsibility to take control of their own destiny. They determine their own economic development; they have a knack for seeking out business opportunities and making them a personal priority. If you've been selling for more than a month, you know you do this, too. VITO's personal self-determination is the same as VITO's business determination. VITO *is* VITO, Inc. I have not found this to be the case with other players at VITO, Inc. In fact, most of them have less in common with VITO on this front than you do. When you're talking to an important prospect or customer, do you say things like:

> » I'm sorry, that's not my area of responsibility.
> » I don't control that policy.
> » There's not much I can do about that.

Or are you far more likely to say:

> » Let me see what I can do about that.
> » I'll take care of that for you.
> » Here's what I can do for you.

I currently own this trait, or will own it by the time I finish this book. (Yes/No)

6. I Focus to Completion

The most successful VITOs and their organizations have a habit of completion. Most of the stuff they start gets done. Whether it gets the desired result or fails to make the mark, VITO makes sure it crosses the finish line. Here's one big reason: VITO writes down goals, plans, and objectives! (You do that, too, right?)

I currently own this trait, or will own it by the time I finish this book. (Yes/No)

7. I Have Integrity

Do you do what you say you'll do, when you say you'll do it? It doesn't matter what the promise is; it could be sending information, returning a call, paying a bill (on time), showing up for a in-person meeting (on time), or returning a book to the library (on time). VITOs are more likely than anyone else in the organization to make sure they actually do what they say they'll do. If something goes wrong and they aren't able to follow through on a commitment, they're the first ones to let you know. So, do you pick up the phone and let your new customers know that their delivery is going to be late or short of a particular item? If you're running even a minute late, do you call your prospect and let them know . . . without an excuse? (As in, "I'll be a few minutes late because of the traffic.")

I currently own this trait, or will own it by the time I finish this book. (Yes/No)

8. I Am a Team Player

When I was a salesperson at Hewlett Packard, I was fortunate to win many awards for my sales performance. On those special occasions, I would take the plaque or trophy to a local engraving shop and have the names of my support team emblazoned on the item. Then I would bring it into the office and pass it around to the team members. Not one of those trophies ever made it to my own desk. Here's my point: My personal observations of VITOs is that they are very good at building a powerful, capable, loyal team . . . and then they go about taking care of that team. Most VITOs are far more likely to put the spotlight on their team than they are on themselves.

I currently own this trait, or will own it by the time I finish this book. (Yes/No)

9. I Am Optimistic and Upbeat

Notice that VITOs surround themselves with can-do people. There's a good reason for this: Successful VITOs do not dwell on what's happening to them, but rather on how to *react* to what's happening. That's a big part of the inner circle's job: Keeping the focus on what can happen, not on what can't happen (or what didn't happen). Smart VITOs never stop asking themselves, "How can I help this person win, and in the process create a win for me and my organization? What's the best possible outcome I can create with what's in front of me?" Smart VITOs look at what everyone else looks at but see something different.

I currently own this trait, or will own it by the time I finish this book. (Yes/No)

10. I Am Interested in Problem Solving

Success in sales requires that you are truly interested in helping someone solve a problem. The greatest companies in the world, run by the greatest VITOs in the world, know this. Problem solving requires that you be truly interested in the other person and their current and/or future situation, and that you be fully present for every conversation, without prejudice or impatience. VITO specialize in this. Do you? If you have any doubts about this, ask a current customer these questions: "If you were to describe me and my company to someone else in your industry, what would it sound like? What would you say we do?"

I currently own this trait, or will own it by the time I finish this book. (Yes/No)

11. I Approach My Life and My Work with a Sense of Purpose

Like VITO, you must be on a mission. VITOs are intentional in their position and purpose; they didn't just happen to become the CEO. They don't just show up for work every day. They are absolutely certain about *why* they're doing *what* they're doing. When you are certain about your purpose, your work effort is more focused, and that focus brings greater results. You are more energized, and that energy brings greater results. VITO knows: *"Why do I love what I do all day?"* You'd better know it, too! (Trust me, some variation on this question will come up during one of your conversations with VITO.)

I currently own this trait, or will own it by the time I finish this book. (Yes/No)

12. I Am Resourceful Enough to Dig for the Strategies, Resources, and Answers I Need

VITOs are exceptionally, sometimes miraculously, resourceful. VITOs are able to respond quickly and effectively, especially in difficult situations. They have the ability to be creative in problem solving, to think (and act) outside the box, more or less instantaneously. They know that there is almost always more than one right answer to a question, and they specialize in asking themselves and others questions like these:

> » Is there another way to get what we want?
> » Is the desired result really the best result under the current circumstances?
> » Who else has information that might help us/me overachieve the mission?
> » What other resources do we have that can help?
> » Might there be something very similar to what we need that might also work?
> » Who on our team are the experts in this area?
> » Who in the marketplace is an expert in this area?
> » What is one more action/idea/step that we can consider?
> » What would someone I respect do in this same situation?
> » What would my biggest competitor do in this same situation?
> » What is the number-one player in this area doing?
> » Has this problem/situation ever been resolved by anyone else before?

I currently own this trait, or will own it by the time I finish this book. (Yes/No)

Are You Twelve for Twelve?

If you're able to answer yes to all twelve of these questions, then congratulations: You either now have or soon will have what it takes to establish and maintain Equal Business Stature with VITO.

Once you've got that, anything and everything is possible. For instance . . .

ASK VITO THE TOUGH QUESTIONS!

Prove that you have Equal Business Stature. Get in the habit of asking VITO the tough questions. Be prepared to hear a direct answer (one that you may not want to hear). You must be able to respond directly to each and every possible answer you get! For example:

You: Ms. Importanta, could you see yourself becoming one of our customers by the end of this month?

VITO: Maybe.

You: What would it take for you to change your answer from "Maybe" to "Yes"?

Chapter 9

The Principles of VITO Marketing

What do we mean when we say "marketing?" What about the words "sales," "advertising," and "public relations"? How do these disciplines connect to our efforts to connect with VITO? To answer these questions, we need to get clear on some important definitions.

Advertising

Advertising is bringing a product, service, or solution to the attention of potential suspects, prospects, and existing customers. Advertising is typically focused on one particular product, service, and/or solution; an advertising plan for one product might be very different than one for another product. Advertising can be carried out by means of a variety of media, including all-important person-to-person contact.

Marketing

Marketing describes the wide range of research and activities designed to make sure you're meeting the ongoing and changing needs of your suspects, prospects, and customers. Marketing, too, is usually focused on one product, service, or solution. A marketing plan for one product might be very different than one for another product. Marketing activities typically includes research to find out what groups of potential suspects, prospects, and existing customers exist, what their needs are, which of those needs you can meet, and how you should meet them. It also includes analyzing the competition, positioning your (new or existing) product, service or solution, and pricing. Marketing also includes promotional efforts undertaken through various media that overlap with the disciplines of advertising, public relations, and sales.

Public Relations

Public relations (also known as PR) typically include ongoing activities to ensure the overall company and its brand has a strong and positive public image. PR activities generally include helping the targeted public understand the company, its mission, its values, its priorities, and, last but not least, its products, services, and solutions. PR is generally conducted through media such as newspapers, television, magazines, online portals, social networks, and other media, including person-to-person contact.

Sales

Sales typically involve cultivating suspects and prospects in a market, conveying the benefits and value of a particular product, service or solution to the suspect(s) and prospect(s), determining whether what you're offering them fits their needs, and then eventually closing the sale by exchanging their money for your products, services, and/or solutions.

VITO RULE #15	Selling to VITO (also known as picking up the phone and calling VITO) is marketing, advertising, public relations, and sales all at the same time!

It's your job to combine advertising, marketing, PR, and sales in a one-on-one approach to VITO. When you're with VITO and the Decision Maker(s), you'll be actively engaged in the art of selling, even if you're out on the golf course, sitting at a table having lunch, or on a tour of one of their facilities. If you should find yourself in a conversation with Seemore or the Recommender, then, by definition, you're not actively engaged in selling. Why not? *All together now:* Because neither Seemore nor the Recommender can buy anything!

For the balance of this chapter, we're going to synchronize your organization's advertising, marketing, and PR efforts with your sales skills to effectively sell to VITO. What you'll find is that if it's good for VITO it will be good for the Decision Maker. Later on in the book, I'll give you some tips on how to initiate the process of exploring, discovering, uncovering, and understanding the perceived needs, problems, and desires of the Seemores and Recommenders of the world. But for now, please forget that Seemore and the Recommender exist. What you're about to learn *will not* work with them.

Pulling It All Together

What if we could take your organization's ads, marketing, PR, and sales pitches, and pull from all that stuff only what is important to

VITO? What if we could then translate that stuff into the language of VITO, then put everything in one, easy-to-read, direct, and to-the-point page? What if we could send that page directly to every VITO in your sales territory who would be predisposed to buy your products, services, and solutions? And what if, having done all that, then you picked up the phone and called VITO? The result would be a one-way ticket to Sales Heaven. Track down the following stuff right now:

> » The most recent ads your organization has been running. Don't forget online pop-ups, banner ads, direct mail, and trade journals.
> » The most recent marketing intelligence your company has put together, including but not limited to, research, surveys, competitive analysis, marketplace and industry information.
> » The most recent press releases from your organization. (Go back at least six months if possible.)
> » The most recent press releases from the ten companies you would most like to sell to right now. (Again, go back at least six months if possible.)

Here comes the fun part. Just to set your expectations, what you're about to do will take you about thirty minutes. It will be time very well spent! When you're done, you will have the launching platform necessary to create the approach that will allow you to sell to VITO.

Step One

You'll recall that, in an earlier chapter, I outlined the four results that VITO is eager to overachieve. These four desired outcomes are common to virtually all VITOs.

Here they are again:

1. Increasing revenues and exceeding the projected revenue plan
2. Increasing efficiencies and effectiveness of:
   » Revenue-generating employees
   » Mission-critical employees
   » Mission-critical processes
   » Workflow and related operations
   » Procurement
   » Capital resources
   » Customer-facing services
3. Cutting and or containing costs and moving away from unpredictable expenses to accurate and forecasted budgets
4. Staying in compliance and operating well within corporate culture and any state and or federal agency and governmental regulations

Now, pull out a yellow highlighter. Take your company's ads, marketing materials, and press releases and highlight the words, phrases, graphs, charts, and anything else that directly relates to the four results listed above for your ideal customer.

Step Two

Pull out a red pen. Take out the press releases of each of the companies you would like to turn into customers that are a) in your territory and b) in your target niche. Use your red pen to circle or underline the words, phrases, graphs, charts, and captions that relate in any way to the VITO outcomes listed in Step One.

Please don't skip over this step!

What did you find out? Here's my guess: You have several areas in red that directly overlap with the stuff you highlighted in yellow, stuff that your company can do.

Step Three

Whatever you do, don't skip this! This step, too, is essential. We're going find out how what you've already been delivering to your existing customers can be quantified into one of two important VITO Value categories.

Category A: Hard Dollar Value

What specific results, measured in numbers and/or percentages, have you delivered to your existing marketplace(s)/industry(ies) in the areas listed in Step One?

For instance, have you been able to increase revenues by some number or percentage? Have you decreased time to market by a certain number of days? Have you cut the time (by some specific number of days) necessary to process Accounts Payables? Have you reduced some fixed expense by a certain percentage?

All of what I've mentioned here falls into the category of Hard Dollar Value achievements. I want you to list at least three such achievements in the space below for each marketplace(s) or industry(ies) you have existing customers in. Don't even think about jumping ahead to the next chapter until you've completed this!

Category B: Soft Dollar Value

What results have you delivered to your existing marketplace(s)/ industry(ies) in the areas that are listed in Step One that you can't measure with a number and/or a percentage? These are results that you articulate using descriptive words and/or phrases like:

- » Greater brand recognition
- » Improved employee morale
- » Dramatically improved customer services
- » Obtaining full compliance with government regulation
- » Better community relations

Got it? Now, list at least three Soft Dollar Value results in the space below for each marketplace(s) or industry(ies) where you have customers. Don't even think about jumping ahead to the next chapter until you've completed this!

| |
| |
| |

You'll recall we used a mind-jogger illustration of your stuff doing a mysterious disappearing act and the result or impact that would have. You may want to revisit it to help you refine what you just wrote.

Step Four

What you'll need to do now is take your most impressive Hard Dollar Value and your most impressive Soft Dollar Value and create a statement that is the narrative or summary of those two value statements. When you create this statement *do not* use your company name, product name, or product number. Stick to the words and phrases that you've highlighted in both red and yellow in the materials you marked up in Steps One and Two.

Here's what your statement could look like:

Increase shareholder economics with up to [27 percent]
greater [cash on hand,] while cutting up to [$60,000] of
[annual expense]—without compromising compliance or
marketplace credibility.

Here's what your statement *shouldn't* look like:

Our newest line of linked-sequential servers will consume less
power take up less footprint and have 97.3 percent uptime on
average with a wide array of platform applications software,
network enrichment resources, and spyware support.

Now, create your thirty-word statement in the box below. Don't go any further until you've got your thirty-word statement created!

Step Five:

Earlier in this chapter I mentioned the word "predisposed" when talking about approaching the VITOs in your sales territory. Now, pull up your current sales forecast and look at the prospects that you've already started your sales process with and ask yourself this question: "Would any of the VITOs in these accounts be interested in what I've just written?"

Next, look at your list of existing customers and ask yourself this question: "Would any of the VITOs in these accounts be interested in what I've just written?"

If you answered yes to either (or both) of these questions, turn the page quickly and go on to the next chapter.

If you answered no to both of these questions, take a break. Once you've had enough time to recharge your batteries, give yourself the chance to work your way through all the steps in this chapter more carefully than you did this time. Unfortunately, you missed something . . . and you're not yet ready to launch your marketing, advertising, public relations, and sales campaign for VITO! Not to worry. Once you're able to confidently answer yes, you'll be ready to take advantage of the rest of this book.

Chapter 10

VITO's Time

If there's one thing VITOs all around the world agree on, it's that their time is too valuable to waste.

I've been selling to VITO for the past three decades, and at times, I have thought the world's VITOs must surely have been trained by the same "executive coach" on how to let everyone know how precious time is to them and how busy they are! Here are some of the more popular responses:

> » I've got lots to do . . . what's on your mind?
> » You've caught me leaving for a meeting . . . what do you want?
> » I don't have a lot of time, so what do you want from me?
> » Let's get started . . . I've got to run to another meeting in less than five minutes.
> » Go ahead . . . I'll just sign these papers while you show me what you've got.
> » I am too busy for this.
> » Today's your lucky day . . . you've got the CEO on the phone. What do you want from me?

I've learned from experience that when you show VITO that you respect and honor his or her time, and prove that *your* time is equally important to *you*, you'll be *granted enough of VITO'S time to discuss what you need to discuss.* The opposite is also true. If you waste VITO's time and act like yours isn't worth much, you won't get the time or the sale you're after.

So how do you prove without a shadow of a doubt that you have the utmost respect for the time-compressed world in which VITO lives in?

Start by accepting the reality *of VITO's available time window for your first written message.*

VITO RULE #16 When you create any written correspondence that you want VITO to actually process, you'll have to make it a fast read. A fast read in VITO's world means thirty seconds.

Yes, I said thirty seconds. If you don't hit that target, it's "round file" time. You probably need a moment for that one to sink in, right? Take a few seconds and catch your breath.

Welcome Back!

Here are some other realities that connect to VITO's (narrow) time window.

If you want VITO to attend any type of presentation at all (in person, web-based, remote video, whatever) you'll have to compress your thoughts and visuals as if you were showing them to someone with a severe case of ADD. If you don't, VITO will simply check out—mentally, physically, or both.

When you're finally on the phone with VITO, you'll have less than three seconds to break preoccupation and snag the intentional area of VITO's brain. You read right: *three seconds*. If you don't hit that target, you'll hear a click and dial tone.

When you're in person with VITO, you'll have less than thirty seconds of face time to prove that whatever time you've asked for will actually be granted. If you don't, your "scheduled" meeting will instantly abort. If you want to get a second appointment with VITO, you'll have to prove in some way, shape, or form that you can deliver value faster than anyone else can in your space. If you don't, you'll never see VITO in person again.

Believe it, those are the real-world time frames you have to work with. I know they're intimidating the first time you come across them, but they're the price you must pay for entering VITO's world. Stick with me, and I'll show you how to hit them and make the most of them.

First, some specifics.

If You Want VITO to "Lean Into" Your Phone Call . . .

. . . You must break preoccupation and snag VITO's attention within roughly the first *twelve words* of the conversation.

Again, I am not kidding. I'm assuming that you're talking to a VITO on the East Coast of the United States. If you're calling a West Coast VITO, you've got till about fifteen words.

Here's how the behind-quota salesperson with a zip code in Sales Hell usually opens the call with VITO:

"Hello, Ms. Importanta, how are you today? Great . . . hey, did I catch you at a good time? The purpose of my call today is to let you know . . . ."

Notice: This person is toast *before* he or she gets to explain the purpose of the call.

If You Want VITO to Read any Written Correspondence . . .

. . . You'll need to get your point across in *thirty words or less*. You'll put more effort, care, and attention into those thirty words than most salespeople put into their whole presentation. But the effort will be worth it.

I'll show you how to find the right words (and where to put them) later on in the book. For now, understand that the days of multiple-page letters, "long copy," and long, rambling conclusions to your presentations are over. That stuff might work for Seemore, but it won't work for VITO.

If You Want VITO to Attend any Type of Presentation . . .

. . . You will only have three slides to show to VITO.

You will only put a maximum of fifteen words on each slide.

You will talk for no more than thirty seconds on each slide.

You will order your slides as follows:

» Slide 1: The results VITO can expect and the "time to value." (This is the slide you are probably used to putting *last*. Get used to the new sequence. VITO needs to see this *first*.)

» Slide 2: The resources VITO must spend . . . be it time, money, and or talent.

> » Slide 3: Social proof about who else in a similar industry is achieving similar results and or your guarantee.

If You Want VITO to Remember Your Message for More Than about Ninety Seconds, Regardless of the Medium You Use to Deliver that Message . . .

. . . Then you will concisely cover these four topics, near and dear to VITO's heart, *in this order:*

> » Revenue
> » Effectiveness and efficiencies of all operations
> » Cost reduction without compromising quality
> » Compliance with government and industry requirements

These should look familiar. These are the four desired outcomes VITO is always interested in generating.

If You Want to Leave a Good First Impression with VITO While You're Meeting VITO in Person . . .

. . . You'll do so in less than thirty seconds. That's right, you have thirty precious seconds to make your best first impression. Here's how that same zip-code-in-Sales-Hell salesperson typically opens the face-to-face meeting:

"Mr. Benefito, thanks for taking the time to meet with me today! Before I tell you what we do at Zenity World Products and how we've helped other companies just like yours, I've just got to ask you about that gold-plated golf club hanging on your wall . . . do you play golf?"

That salesperson just ate up twenty-two of those thirty precious seconds, and in the process triggered VITO's exit and the premature ending of this meeting. Never, ever open a meeting with VITO using an "ice-breaker."

You now have four new windows of time to work with. They may seem impossible to you; I assure you that they're not.

In the pages that follow, I will show you *how* you can meet these time windows in a compelling, memorable way to build bridges, and lasting relationships with, VITO.

Before you turn the page, memorize your new "contact" timeframes.

Written correspondence = 30 seconds

Telephone = 3 seconds

Presentations = 3 slides / 15 words / 30 seconds

Never use ice-breakers.

Chapter 11

Exponential Revenue Increases

I hold this truth to be self-evident: No matter what you sell, there is no higher-margin business than repeat business from your existing customers.

Why? Because add-on business doesn't have the high cost of acquisition that new business from a prospect has. In other words, the cost of sales associated with your current customers is much, much lower than the cost of sales associated with brand-new customers.

This principle is no big secret, and most salespeople would probably be able to express it during, say, a job interview. The true secret to success in the realm of sales, I would submit, lies not in your ability to repeat this principle, but in your ability to implement it. Specifically, it lies in your willingness to address this question:

"How can I go about getting all the add-on business I've worked hard for and deserve from my existing customers, and, while I'm at it, take every in-process opportunity I'm currently working on and expand the initial sale amount?"

I realize that's a question you may not have asked and may not have been expecting. All the same, it's a question you will need to address on a personal level if you're serious about building your sales process around VITO. *If and only if you are ready to assume personal accountability for answering this question, please keep reading.*

Let's Rock!

Get out your sales forecast, and while you're at it, grab all of your existing account files. We're about to get to work. (By the way, everything that follows can be adapted to both "hunter" salespeople who are responsible for generating new business and "farmer" salespeople who are responsible for maintaining and growing the business from existing customers.)

Take a look at the names of all of your exiting customers, and while you're scanning the list, be brutally honest with yourself. Do you have all of the add-on business you deserve or just a thin slice?

My guess: *thin slice.* Here's why: The person you're calling on month after month (or year after year) is keeping you a secret—and keeping you in check. This may have been part of your contact's plan all along, to keep you right where you *supposedly* belong. Alternatively, you may have consciously taken the low road when it came to launching on this account, and then become a little complacent about going deeper and wider within this account. Be honest: It's possible, right?

In either case, I've got some very bad news for you. Unless you expand your coverage in this *and every one of your other existing accounts,* you will eventually lose the business. Your bread-and-butter clients will vanish. As a matter of fact, there is a strong possibility that right now, while you're reading these words, your competition is making a call on the person who can, with the snap of a finger, have whatever it is you've sold shoved out the door. How do I know? I speak from experience. Before I started selling to VITO, that's exactly what happened to me!

Keep working. Take a look at the names of all the sales opportunities you currently have in play. Focus on the sales opportunities you expect to close in the next thirty days. Have you uncovered all of the areas in this organization that *could* buy your products, services, and or solutions? Are there other individuals, departments, divisions, or locations that could also use what you have to offer or have you just focused on a thin slice?

I'm guessing that the answer here is *thin slice*, too. Here's why.

The person you initially contacted—yep, the one who you've got listed right there on your forecast as the "decision maker"—isn't really the decision maker at all. Oh, he or she might have told you that, but in all likelihood that person was—what's the phrase I'm looking for here—oh, right: *lying.*

Regardless of his or her formal title, your "decision maker" is almost certainly *not* the person *everything* related to your product or service rolls up to, because he or she is not the person with the ultimate veto power. As a result, you're about to settle for the smaller deal, whether you know it now or not! You're headed for a short sale, a small play. You're on the road to Sales Hell.

Toward Exponential Increases in Your Personal Revenue: Existing Business

If you're pulling a commission check and you want to make more money, I want you to pay very close attention to what follows. As the alumni of my public seminars, private corporate training events, and webinars can attest, the road I'm about to show you is the one that leads directly to Sales Heaven. The people who've walked this road have posted some truly amazing results. These results include the following exponential increases in revenue.

» Up to 120 percent increases in add-on business
» 14 percent reduction in the need to win back customers
» 54 percent increase in the size of the initial sale
» 57 percent increase in referrals

What do these results have in common? Simply put: VITO, the Very Important Top Officer. This is the one person (besides yourself) who can make all of this happen, either in your existing accounts or in the opportunities you currently have in play. Are you ready to make these kinds of exponential increases?

I thought so. What would happen if you took the thirty-word narrative you developed in Chapter 9 and found a way to get it delivered to the presiding VITO in every existing account you now have sitting in front of you? Do you think that VITO would want you to explore all of the possibilities across the entire enterprise?

Yes! Absolutely! No question about it!

Here's a scenario to ponder: Your sales manager, or your organization's own VITO, sends an e-mail, fax, or carrier pigeon message to the VITOs in every single one of your accounts. That message says something like the following:

[Mr. Benefito], your team and my team have been [increasing shareholder value/revenues/margins . . . cutting expenses/increasing efficiencies/improving compliance] by an average of [X percent] for the past [Y] years. We strongly suspect that we could create similar or even greater results in your [shipping and receiving, accounting, operations and marketing departments]. How would you suggest we direct our teams to move forward in the next [XX] days to quickly uncover all of the possibilities?

Notice how we've tied the narrative to the element of time in the final question. By the way, you'll see how we'll be editing this message down to meet the requirements shown on page 96.

By sending this message, would your sales manager, or your organization's own VITO, create some ripples in the pond as far as the relationship you have with your existing contact? Maybe. Maybe not. For a moment, though, I don't want you to worry about that. (Would VITO worry about that?) Instead, I want you to think about this VITO Rule:

VITO RULE #17

VITOs are looking for ways to improve every area of their organization, not just the area you happen to know about and are working with.

Toward Exponential Increases in Your Personal Revenue: New Business

Now I want you to ask yourself what would happen if you were to unveil your own thirty-word narrative to VITO *before you contacted anyone else in all of the new opportunities that are now sitting in front of you.*

The message could be sent in any number of media. I'll walk you through the first of those—the VITO letter—in the next chapter. For now, understand that the heart of the letter you'll be creating might sound like this:

[Mr. Benefito], we have been [increasing revenues/cutting expenses/ increasing efficiencies/improving compliance] for [3 of the top 4] companies in your industry. We strongly suspect that we could create similar or even greater results in your [shipping and receiving, accounting, operations and marketing departments]. How would you suggest we move forward in the next [XX] days to quickly uncover all of the possibilities?

Here again we'll be editing this down . . . you'll see how in just a few chapters.

Now, let's say for a moment that your message resonated with VITO's goals, plans, and objectives for VITO, Inc. What do you think would happen? What do you think the immediate result within VITO, Inc. would be? What do you think VITO would direct his or her Decision Maker(s) to do?

VITO would instruct those Decision Makers to start talking to you and report back with a "reality-check" assessment for his or her personal review, ASAP!

Why? Because VITO is looking for ways to improve every area of their organization, not just the area you happen to know about and work with.

What Do You Do Now?

First, use all the information you've gathered thus far to create a VITO target list reflecting every current customer relationship where you can, want, and deserve to expand your presence.

Then, use all the information you've gathered thus far about your current prospects to create a VITO target list reflecting every piece of new business you want to win more quickly, easily, and profitably.

Make a personal commitment to make maintaining and upgrading *these two lists your life's work!*

Then, turn the page to begin the process of harnessing a force of nature—VITO's desire to improve VITO, Inc.—to deliver exponential revenue increases for your organization and commission dollars for yourself.

Chapter 12

Two Rules for Snagging the Intentional Area of VITO's Brain

I sent 2,400 letters . . . and got 1,600 appointments with VITO!
—Gary B.

Gary is one of my star students, as his eye-popping numbers suggest. In this chapter, I'll teach you how to create a single piece of correspondence that will yield comparable, or perhaps even better, response rates than the ones Gary is enjoying. To begin with, we're talking about that old-fashioned pre-Internet communications medium Gary used to generate such astonishing results: It's known as a letter. As in one piece of paper you'll physically mail to VITO.

Before you start thinking (or saying out loud), "Tony, I don't do letters—they're a waste of time," answer these two questions:

First, what would happen if you could get every qualified VITO in your sales territory to read something that told them exactly how *you* could help them overachieve their goals, plans, and objectives for *this* year?

Second, what would happen if, after each one of those VITOs read your letter, his or her phone rang, and *you* were on the other end of the line?

I'll tell you what would happen: You would be on your way to earning a permanent zip code in Sales Heaven.

In this chapter, you'll learn what I've proven to be the very best way to approach every VITO in your territory—*without* waiting to run an ad during this year's Super Bowl halftime show.

Two Rules You Must Follow to Snag the Intentional Area of VITO's Brain

VITO RULE #18	You must know which VITOs to approach . . . and which not to approach.

Sending a letter to a VITO who has no need (or interest) in what you can do is a total waste of time. Yet each and every day thousands of salespeople make an attempt to get an appointment with a completely *unqualified* VITO! Following my first rule will put an end to this wasteful activity. From this point forward, you will never even think about approaching a VITO who doesn't fit the persona that matches up with that of your very best customers.

The persona of your very best customers is the role and characteristics they have in their respective industry, marketplace, and competitive space. The more you know about the persona of your existing customers, the more accurately you'll be able to select the VITO prospects to approach.

To follow Rule 18, you must establish the persona of your best existing customers. That means you would, at a minimum, need to know the answers to the following twenty-four questions.

(Take the time to answer these questions *right now*. Write your answers on a separate piece of paper. If you have to devote some time for research—or inspired guesswork—to give these questions the best possible answers *today*, then make that investment. Do not skip any one of these questions.)

Questions You Must Be Able to Answer about Your Organization's Best Customers:

» What industry/marketplace are they in?

» What products, services, and solutions do they provide to that industry/marketplace?

» What is their competitive ranking within that industry/marketplace?

» What is the size of their organization (expressed in number of employees, annual revenue, number of locations, or whatever other metric you can measure and apply across the board)?

» How do they create revenue?

» Do they sell directly to that industry/marketplace?

» Are they a local, regional, national, or global provider to that industry/marketplace?

» Do they have a distribution channel?

» Do they have a private label they provide for others to sell?

» What are they doing with what you've sold them?

» What hard value have you delivered?

» How are they measuring it?

» How would *you* measure it?

» What soft value have you delivered?

» How would they describe it?

» How would *you* describe it?

» What process did they use to buy from you?

» Did they perform an exhaustive survey of the marketplace?

» What was on their list of requirements/specifications?

» Did they shop all competitors?

» Did they grind you down on price?
» What was the deciding factor(s) on their purchase from you?
» What were the benefit(s) that got them the most excited about your products, services, and solution?

Still With Me?

Before you go on, *follow through* on the promise you made to maintain and update those lists you created at the end of the last chapter. Take the answers you just created and look at your current sales forecast and:

First: Find the prospects that match the persona you just created and highlight them in some impossible-to-ignore way.

Next: Take the prospects that *don't* match your existing customer persona to a "T" and delete them from your sales forecast!

I know this must sound to you like I am overreacting (especially if you're getting ready to delete all of your prospects because none of them fit this persona). But in all the years that I've been selling and training sales organizations and consulting with the companions they work for, I've seen countless sales vaporize from sales forecasts because the "prospects" just plain weren't a good fit. Unfortunately, this vaporizing usually happened after months or even years of wasted effort, time, and resources trying to fit a square peg into a round hole!

Think back on your own history, and consider what I've just told you. Does it match up with your own experience? In your heart, do you sense I'm right about this? Delete the prospects that don't match your best customer's persona. Do it now.

Now . . . take the prospects that are *still* on your sales forecast and quickly find out what VITO's name is and what his or her Personal Assistant's name is. (If you need some help in knowing how to find out the latter of those two items, no worries, I'll get to that in a little while.)

VITO RULE #19	You must know how to approach VITO.

Within a specific industry or market, the VITOs of your existing customers have precisely the same business interests as the VITOs of your prospects—as long as you make sure your prospects fit the persona of your existing customers to a "T!"

Why write a letter? Because VITOs are readers. On average, they read twenty books a year. Of these, sixteen are professionally related and four are for fun and entertainment. In addition, they typically read the daily newspaper (this could be the *Wall Street Journal* or another, local, business journal) and an untold number of newsletters, internal memos, blogs, and whatever else suits their fancy. Are there non-paper-based variations you can use? Yes. But learn how to write the letter first.

The next thing to remember is: *Keep it short*. Yes, I realize I'm repeating this. Less is always more when you're selling to VITO, and that applies to this correspondence.

Approach VITO by writing a letter that features:

» Short sentences
» Short paragraphs
» One page with lots of white space
» Common language, simple words and phrases
» No words/phrases or terminology that are unfamiliar to VITO

Each and every part of this correspondence must stand on its own. Each and every part of this correspondence must tie into something VITO loves to do. For instance:

VITOs *love to give orders and take action*

Therefore, VITO must be able to forward this correspondence to one of the Decision Makers they hold personally responsible for accomplishing whatever it is that you can help VITO, Inc. overachieve.

VITOs *depend upon their Personal Assistants*

Therefore, VITO must get a recommendation from the Personal Assistant about this correspondence—*or* the Personal Assistant must get the letter onto VITO's radar screen. If there were ever a tightly knit team, it's this one! This correspondence will address VITO's relationship with his or her assistant in a very special and appropriate way.

VITO *has a unique mindset and unique methods*

Therefore, this correspondence must align with everything we have learned about VITO thus far about what VITO likes to do and how VITO likes to do it!

Chapter 13

The Six Elements of VITO Correspondence

I happen to like sending a letter in advance of picking up the telephone and making contact with VITO. Why? Well, this approach creates two very important outcomes for me.

1. It lets VITO know I'll be calling.
2. It puts the VITO call on my calendar and keeps me accountable for doing what most of us salespeople just hate to do—prospect for new business!

If you're like me and you need a good dose of self-discipline, you're going to love this chapter! (And if you're curious about what kind of sales letter makes you schedule prospecting time on your own personal calendar, read on!)

VITO RULE #20 Every piece of VITO correspondence has six specific parts, each of which must stand on its own but also be logically connected to all the other parts.

Here's a quick rundown on the six parts that make up a VITO letter.

Element One: A Headline

This headline breaks VITO's preoccupation and earns attention and readership. It's short, to the point, and will not include words or phrases with which VITO is unfamiliar. It is similar to the headlines VITO might read in a business newspaper or magazine. The headline is short (less than thirty words), hard hitting, and attention grabbing.

Element Two: A Tie-In Paragraph

This paragraph is designed to connect the headline to the rest of the correspondence; typically, it introduces some kind of social proof for the claim just made. Social proof is evidence of your track record with other VITOs in a similar or identical industry as the VITO you're sending this correspondence to.

Element Three: Benefit Bullets

This is a series of short statements of your abilities in the areas of greatest interest to this VITO. Whenever you are in doubt about what the areas of interest for a given VITO might be, just follow the priority list I've already shared with you as your default setting.

1. Increasing top-line revenues
2. Increasing the effectiveness of revenue-generating employees, mission-critical employees, and mission-critical processes

3. Cutting expenses
4. Becoming fully compliant with any and all government regulations or industry practices

Element Four: An Ending Paragraph

This is where you state a call to action or introduce some level of suspicion as to what the possibilities could be. You could also invite VITO to engage certain Decision Makers—by name—in this paragraph. Yep, this requires some additional work. You know why you should do it anyway? Because it works like a charm.

Hey, guess what? Even though this is the ending paragraph . . . we're not done yet!

Element Five: An Action-Oriented Postscript

This is where you'll put the precise day, date, and time that you'll be calling VITO. In this postscript, you'll include the name of VITO's personal assistant.

Element Six: A Short Handwritten Note

You will attach this to the back (not the front) of your correspondence. It's a note to VITO's personal assistant. You know he or she's going to be opening up all of VITO's mail and reading this, right?

Examples of All Six Elements

Before I show you an entire letter, I'm going to give you some examples of each of the elements. I've gone into my archives of over 25,000 letters and selected my favorite pieces. Of course, if what you're about to read matches up with the personas and results of your customers and prospects—use it! In the far more likely event that what you read in this isn't tightly focused on your world, you will need to make the necessary changes. All words in [brackets] will, in all likelihood, need to be tailored to your specific situation.

Ready? Here's the ultimate highlight reel showing off my favorite elements of my favorite kind of letter—the VITO letter.

My Favorite Headlines

The most powerful headlines are ones that will catch VITO's attention and get VITO to think (or say aloud), "How did they do that?" or "I would love to talk with this genius." Headlines can include a quote from your VITO, which should be easy to get, or one of your existing customer's VITOs, which is almost as easy to get.

"The world's largest electronic manufacturer increased stock value and reduced time-to-market by [63] days while eliminating [$87.9 million in unnecessary inventory]. My team led the way in just [144] days."

Note: You can eliminate the need for a direct quote and all the numbers—except the time it took to pull it off—and still get the point across. For instance:

"Further increase shareholder wealth while at the same time achieving greater compliance—in just [144 days]. Here's the team that helped do it."

STOP! Did you notice how each of the examples I just shared with you showed VITO that you have evaluated *both sides* of the risk equation—both the immediate payoff (which any salesperson can talk about) and the likely implications of taking a new step (which very few salespeople even consider)? You're not just sharing a story about increasing shareholder value; you're sharing a story about increasing shareholder value *while at the same time reducing time-to-market and eliminating unnecessary inventory costs.* You're not just sharing a story about increasing shareholder wealth; you're sharing a story about increasing sharcholder *wealth while at the same time improving compliance.*

This is called a *balanced gain equation,* and it's an extremely important part of any benefit you discuss with, or preview for, VITO. You must look at all sides of the equation, just as VITO must!

Some More Examples

"Further improve operational economics, compliance, and globalization capabilities, in just [90 days]."

"Further improve shareholder wealth in the next [six months] by improving revenues while lowering expenses."

"Further increase shareholder value by more effective operation of revenue-generating assets while cutting up to [31 percent] in fixed cost, in just [6] months."

"Board Members . . . help create a Center of Excellence, expand service lines and referrals, while improving medical staff recruitment and retention."

"Reduce hospital mortality up to [29 percent] while cutting critical nursing staff turnover by as much as [33 percent]."

"A 'top ten' advertising firm increased net working capital by [$76.5M] while improving office efficiency by [21 percent], in just [three months]. These are proven results based upon our repeatable process."

"Our business partnership has delivered [$1.4 million] in increased revenue and reduced expenses by [$6 million] annually. We accomplished this for a CEO in your industry."

"One of the world's largest electronic manufacturers reduced cycle time by [44 days] while eliminating [$3.1 million] in inventory. They accomplished this within [90 days] of using my team's ideas."

"This year, one of the top three U.S. oil companies will increase their margins while reducing operating expenses by [$15,900 per month], as a direct result of my team's ideas."

"By taking my team's advice, a major U.S. automaker increased one division's revenue by [200 percent] while saving [$457,000 annually]."

"One of the largest telecommunications companies in America has increased the efficiency and effectiveness of their employees while realizing an annual savings of over [$1,200,444]. How can my team serve you?"

My Favorite Tie-In Paragraphs

The best tie-in paragraphs are ones that keep the ball rolling and add a new thought for VITO to process. In some cases, this new thought can provide a segue into Element Three, your benefit bullets.

WARNING: It's very important *not* to repeat anything in your tie-in paragraph that you said in your headline. Repeated words, phrases, and ideas will turn VITO off.

Here come the examples.

"We've helped [cut time] and [expense] into extremely effective business tools while enhancing our customer's ability to [concentrate on core competencies]. We've accomplished this in one or more of the following ways:"

"During the past [12 years], we have worked with [29] [manufacturing companies] collectively, and we've been able to [increase margins and shareholder value]. Are any of the following achievements on your list of goals, plans, or objectives for the [first half] of this calendar [year]? If so, the good news is that we have created a proven, repeatable process that we guarantee to deliver results such as:"

"While you peruse this correspondence, [12] other [CEOs] in your industry are benefiting from our innovations with [higher margins], [lower expenses], and [greater peace of mind]. Here are [two] additional results we are providing our business partners:"

My Favorite Benefit Bullets

The best benefit bullets are short and to the point. Here, again, be careful not to repeat anything. Notice that in some of the benefit bullets that follow, I've added an advantage to the list of benefits. (A side note: Your benefit bullets could also take the form of a chart or graph.)

Roll the highlight reel!

» Reduction of annual variable cost by as much as $6.4 million without compromising patient care.
» Up to 30 percent increase in patient billings while maintaining full compliance and fiduciary responsibilities.
» Further improve clinical results including up to 54 percent decrease in hospital mortality.
» Lowering inventory and improving product availability by detecting supply disruptions early and responding with cost-effectiveness in mind.
» Increased revenues of up to [44 percent] per year have been reported by our clients.

» Discovering and responding to trends that become visible with a deeper understanding of supplier, inventory, and shipment knowledge-based information.

» Protect Market Share—Employee and client satisfaction & retention consistently adds up to better utilization of human assets. Consider what an employee turnover of only [8 percent] and customer churn of less than [14 percent] does for top, middle, and bottom-line numbers.

» Greater add-on business potential while reducing expenses by as much as [$258,000] each month!

» Our partnership improves return on assets by actually reducing the asset base while at the same time making the balance of this base perform to extreme levels of efficiency.

» Faster product shipments by as much as [65 days]. Improved net working capital equals increased inventory turns and minimizes lost sales opportunities to competition.

» Customer satisfaction is higher because the information they receive is more accurate, relevant, and timely.

My Favorite Ending Paragraphs

The ending paragraph is where you want to make a clear call to action *or* introduce some level of doubt and suspicion about whether you can deliver these kinds of results for VITO, Inc. If you choose the latter option, you'll be dialing into VITO's powerful competitive nature, need to win, and desire not to miss out on anything!

Here come some real gems.

"[Ms. Importanta], the possibility for your company to achieve similar or even greater results is difficult to determine at this point.

One fact is certain: You are the one person who can initiate the call to action, and together, our team of experts can quickly explore exactly what all the possibilities are."

"[Mr. Benefito], what does this have to do with your [financial institute]? Perhaps everything, if you determine that one or more of the results mentioned in this correspondence are relevant to your strategic initiatives for the balance of this [calendar year]. All that's necessary is for you to consider taking my call."

"[Mr. Benefito], it's obvious you know your institute's challenges better than anyone does. But what may not be so obvious is how [YOUR COMPANY NAME HERE], the [world leader in business solutions], could help you realize similar or even greater results before the end of the [first half of this year]. If you would like to take the first step, our complete team of [business experts] can quickly determine each and every possibility."

My Favorite Action-Oriented Post Scripts

This is the shortest part of your correspondence, but it may well have the greatest impact. Why? You're including VITO's Personal Assistant in the conversation, and you're also taking the initiative by suggesting a specific day, date, and time for your first conversation. Note that *both of these steps are mandatory.*

I call VITO's Personal Assistant by the gender-neutral name Tommie. Take a look at how powerful this kind of P.S. can be as a conclusion to your letter for either VITO or Tommie. (I say "conclusion," but it's worth noting here that both VITO and Tommie are very likely to scan down quickly to the bottom part of sheet and read this part after the headline catches their intention.)

"P.S. I'll call your office on [Thursday, May 14, at 9:30 A.M.]. If this is an inconvenient time, please have [Tommie] inform me as to when I should make the call. Or, if you like, you can reach me [Monday or Tuesday between 9:00 A.M. and 2:00 P.M.]. I look forward to our conversation."

"P.S. [Tommie], I'll plan on calling your office on [Thursday, May 14, at 9:30 A.M.]. If this isn't a convenient time to have a brief conversation with [Ms. Importanta]. please call me and let me know."

"P.S. The topics of this letter may be important to both of our organizations. That's why I'll plan on calling your office on [Thursday, May 14. at 9:30 A.M.]. If this is an inconvenient time, please have Tommie inform me as to when I should make the call."

My Favorite Handwritten Notes to VITO's Personal Assistant

Building rapport with Tommie is absolutely critical if you expect to gain access to VITO. By including this personal note, you'll be quietly and sincerely saluting Tommie's uniform.

I like to use a yellow sticky note for this special message. Again, it goes on the *back* of the VITO letter.

"[Tommie], your guidance and insights into your enterprise are priceless. As you know, it's so difficult to find a compassionate ear in our busy day and hectic schedules. I'll look forward to our conversation on and finding out what you think about the enclosed correspondence. If you would like to change the time I've suggested, just give me a call."

"[Tommie], please take a look at this correspondence and let me know what your thoughts are about the proven ideas we have for the *[hospitality] industry. If I've selected an inconvenient time for our first conversation, please let me know."*

"[Tommie], we can actually deliver much, much more than is mentioned in this correspondence! So, if it's okay with you, a quick conversation will help me get on the right track and stay there! If the time that I've selected isn't convenient, please let me know."

Six Elements, One Powerful Piece of Correspondence

On the next page, you'll see an example of what this correspondence looks like when you put it all together.

The world's largest electronic manufacturer increased stock value and reduced time-to-market by 63 days while eliminating $87.9 million in unnecessary inventory. My team led the way in just 144 days.

May 12, 20XX

Ms. Importanta
President

During the past 12 years, we have worked with 29 manufacturing companies collectively, and we've been able to increase margins and shareholder value. Are any of the following achievements on your list of goals, plans, or objectives for the first half of this calendar year? If so, the good news is that we have created a proven, repeatable process that we guarantee to deliver results such as:

> Reduction of annual variable cost by as much as $6.4 million without compromising patient care

> Up to 30 percent increase in patient billings while maintaining full compliance and fiduciary responsibilities

> Lowering inventory and improving product availability by detecting supply disruptions early and responding with cost-effectiveness in mind.

Ms. Importanta, the possibility for your company to achieve similar or even greater results is difficult to determine at this point. One fact is certain: You are the one person who can initiate the call to action, and together, our team of experts can quickly explore exactly what all the possibilities are.

To greater success!
Will Prosper
ABC Corp.
760-555-1212

P.S. I'll call your office on Thursday, May 14, at 9:30 A.M. If this is an inconvenient time, please have Tommie inform me as to when I should make the call. Or, if you like, you can reach me Monday or Tuesday between 9:00 A.M. and 2:00 P.M. I look forward to our conversation.

Oh, before I forget: The fact that you're holding this book in your hands entitles you to one full month of my live mentoring. During that time, I'll be able to critique your VITO correspondence personally! To take advantage of this FREE one-on-one coaching, go to page 229 in this book, where you'll find out how to sign up for free. But, don't do it now. Keep moving! Go on to the next chapter.

Chapter 14

Delivering the Message—
Your Telephone Opening
Statement to VITO

There it sits . . . just where you saw it yesterday . . . the 3,000-pound telephone.

Strange, it hasn't rung once all week. Maybe there's something screwy with the phone line?

If there is one topic connected to selling to VITO that is simultaneously challenging, interesting, dramatic, and potentially life changing for each and every one of the people who take my Selling to VITO course, it's the inescapable responsibility of picking up the receiver and actually calling VITOs!

Yes, it is a responsibility. It's also a privilege. It's something you have to hold yourself accountable for. Fortunately, it's a lot easier than you think.

I could tell you story after story of my own experiences with this all-important task. I could tell you story after story about how my alumni have soared to success by using what you're about to learn— and landing VITO appointments for themselves. None of those stories would really matter, though. What's important here is your past experience and whether you are willing to allow it to stand in the way of implementing what you're about to learn.

Before we get started, let me remind you of a couple of promises.

Promise One: As I told you at the outset of this book, I will not teach you, or tell you, to do anything that I am not doing myself. In other words, you are not a member of my private test group! The day that I stop making my own VITO calls is the day I'll stop writing books and teaching seminars about precisely how to do it.

Promise Two: What you're about to learn is both ethical and doable.

A Memorable VITO Call

I will never forget the morning I reached out (by telephone) to VITO, the Chairman of the Board at CompanyYou'dRecognize, and his personal assistant, Alice. Both VITO and Alice were receptive to my opening statement. However, they were skeptical that their sales-people—who were mostly fully degreed, chemical engineers—would have what it takes to sell to VITO. VITO wanted me to do a pilot with all of his vice presidents. "If you can get them to do it," he told me during that first conversation, "my sales team will follow their lead."

That was what I wanted to hear.

VITO's global sales team was 260 strong; his VP team consisted of twelve well-educated, experienced, highly capable professionals. Our pilot class with the VPs was held in Utah in the dead of winter. Why? Because VITO was an avid, accomplished skier with a retreat located smack dab in the middle of the mountains . . . and a private jet to take him there whenever he wanted. That's why. VITO wanted to be close to the skiing! It worked for VITO, so it worked for his VPs and me.

During the very first hour of my pilot class, a particular VP said, "Tony, if you think I am going to pick up the phone and call the CEO of Dupont, you're nuts! Besides, he'll never take my call!"

I remember thinking silently to myself that this wasn't the best way to start a class.

Actually, though, looking back, I realize that it was exactly what we needed to set the stage for one of the most successful roll outs of Selling to VITO ever. Here's why: That VP was brave enough to acknowledge his fear of calling a VITO of a very high-profile organization. And despite his opening comment, this VP was eager to hear what my process was all about.

After the class, we scheduled a VITO Blitz Day (that's a day devoted completely to VITO prospecting, in which I personally assist the individuals making the phone calls to VITO). The day started with each of the VPs identifying the organizations he or she was going to call that day. Guess what? By coincidence, that VP who in the first hour of the program said he'd never call the head of Dupont drew Dupont for his hit list!

Guess what? He did actually pick up the phone and call the CEO of Dupont!

Guess what? The CEO of Dupont picked up his phone totally unprotected by any gatekeepers!

Guess what? The VP actually talked with the CEO of Dupont!

No, he never sold to Dupont—but that's not the point.

AN UNEXPECTED PROBLEM

Scott was at 60 percent of quota (year to date) and working for one of the largest telecom companies in the world when he took my Selling to VITO course. Shortly after the course, he was at his desk making cold calls—to VITO. Paul, the Director of Sales, walked by and noticed that Scott was in his cube early. The following dialogue ensued:

Paul: Morning, Scott! Making some VITO calls?

> *Scott:* Yes, I sure am.
>
> *Paul:* How's it going?
>
> *Scott:* I just got through to a president.
>
> *Paul:* Great! How did it go?
>
> *Scott:* I got so nervous when I heard his voice, I hung up!

My Favorite Personal VITO Call Story

One day, years ago, I had scheduled myself to make ten VITO calls. On my very first call of the day—to the president of the third-largest computer company in the world—VITO picked up the phone, completely unprotected by any gatekeeper!

I was so surprised to hear VITO's voice that, without thinking, I said, "Oh, what a surprise! I expected to get Tommie!"

VITO's response was quick and to the point: "Hold on. Let me get her for you." With a click, he was gone forever. File it under "one big lost VITO conversation opportunity"!

Learn the lessons from these three very different true stories:

> » Whether you think you can't or you think you can, you're right.
> » VITOs (no matter how big or small) will take your call.
> » VITOs (no matter how big or small) will and sometimes do answer their own phones.

And perhaps most important of all . . .

VITO RULE #21 It's okay to make mistakes . . . because none of this is life threatening.

The "Tale of the Tape"

CompanyYou'dRecognize blew the doors off that VITO Blitz Day, won a boatload of new prospects, and turned the VPs into believers. The whole sales staff became believers, too. And CompanyYou'dRecognize became one of my very best clients.

Scott ended that year over quota because he didn't stop making his VITO calls. However, he did stop hanging up on VITO!

I continue to place my VITO calls—and I continue to make the occasional dumb mistake!

How about You?

What's been your experience with using the telephone to contact your prospects? Do you wind up just leaving voice mail messages, getting shunted to a lower-level person, or worse yet, being blocked by a gatekeeper? Does that happen day after day after day?

If so, I have four words for you: "Dude, change your process!"

Ever wonder what would happen if, instead of doing what you're doing now, you reached out directly to VITO? I thought so. Here's what you can expect:

- » 25 percent of the time, VITO will pick up (yep, unprotected).
- » Half of the balance, VITO's personal assistant will pick up.
- » Remaining half of the balance, you'll get dumped into voice mail.

Stick with me, and I will make sure you have everything you need to prepare yourself for all three outcomes.

Chapter 15

What to Do When VITO Picks Up the Phone

VITO—the CEO, president, or owner—is sitting at the desk. It's a busy day. Lots of stuff is going on. VITO is signing checks, shaking hands, patting backs, looking at financial reports, and so on. The phone rings, and Tommie isn't around to answer it. VITO will never, ever let the phone ring without someone answering it, and in this case, that someone is VITO.

What's likely to happen? We'll, if you're prepared with your opening statement, you're going to have a conversation with VITO. Let's start by reviewing what VITO will not tolerate from you.

Twelve Situations VITO Will Not Tolerate
1. Long, drawn-out monologues
2. Stupid questions that you should already know the answer to
3. Uncertainty as to what you want
4. Words and phrases that are unfamiliar
5. Wasting VITO's precious time
6. Unfamiliarity with VITO's industry/niche
7. Any lack of confidence
8. Any kind of BS

9. Ego-based statements of any kind
10. Any mention of VITO's competition
11. Any claims without evidence
12. Mispronouncing VITO's name

You didn't really want to go to any of those (dumb) places during this call, did you?

Now, let's look at what VITO expects.

VITO's Two Expectations

1. Valuable content. Namely:
   » Something VITO doesn't already know
   » Something VITO wants to overachieve
   » Something said in a way that VITO easily understands
   » Apparent knowledge about VITO's industry
   » Some knowledge about VITO's company
   » Clarity on the outcome you want from the call

2. Confident delivery, including:
   » Quick, to-the-point, focused statements
   » A conversational tone
   » You making sure that VITO has plenty of chances to interrupt

Let's Look at Our First Scenario

You just dialed VITO's number. You hear one ring, two rings, three rings, and then . . . VITO picks up!

VITO will say something darn close to, "This is VITO, how can I help you?"

What you say in response will determine the tone of the whole call. Of course, you won't be saying the word "I," your own name, your company's name, or anything equally stupid. Below, you will find a helpful list of . . .

Stupid Things You Will Not Say at This Critical Moment
» "Is this a good time?"
» "Do you have a minute?"
» "I was wondering if . . ."
» "Would you be interested in . . ."
» "I was just making some calls . . ."
» "The purpose of my call is . . ."
» "How are you today?"

Instead of any of those dumb things, you'll say:
"Mr. VITO Benefito?"

That's it. That's all. Stop right there! All you'll be saying to get the conversation going is VITO's name.

Here's the only exception to this: If VITO answers the phone with his/her full name ("VITO Benefito, how can I help you?"), *don't repeat it!* Instead, use their title and company name, like this:

VITO: "VITO Benefito, how can I help you?"
You: "The CEO of VITO, Inc.?"
VITO: "Yep, that's me all right!"

Remember, VITO usually isn't just sitting around waiting for the phone to ring. VITO is busy, and when people are busy, the quickest and most effective way to break the dominant preoccupation is to say the person's name.

Stay formal ("Mr. Vito Benefito") until VITO invites you to use his or her first name. If VITO doesn't say, "Just call me VITO," then you'll continue to address VITO by his or her full and formal name for the duration of the call.

Here's What You'll Say Next

» "It's an honor to finally speak with you . . ."
» "Thanks for picking up the phone."
» "Thanks for taking my call."
» "Thanks for taking the time to talk with me."
» "You're just the person who'll appreciate this."

That's it. That's all. Stop right there! What you just delivered is called a pleasantry. Yes, it's different; yes, it's brief; and yes, when you say it and pause at the end you give VITO a chance to interrupt you and say something like, "Why do you think it's an honor to speak to me?"

When it happens, it's a great way to get started building Equal Business Stature with VITO. You could respond with, "Getting to speak with the CEO of an organization that's had [four consecutive years of double digit growth] is not only an honor but a great opportunity for both of us!"

It's possible, of course, that the conversation might go like this:

VITO: "Who's this?"

You: "Will Prosper, with a thought/idea/topic that may be important to both of us . . ."

Here's What You'll Say Next

"The [CEO] of the world's largest electronic manufacturer increased shareholder value and reduced cycle time by [63] days while eliminating $87.9 million in inventory, in just [144] days."

That's it. That's all. Stop right there!

Okay, let's take a deep breath and look at what we've got. The above response, which I call the Hook, should look familiar to you.

It's the verbal rendition of the headline you put on the top of the VITO correspondence you created a little earlier . . . with one small twist. You added a reference to a title, which is the same title as the VITO you're calling and happen to be talking to right now.

So, if you did happen to send your letter, and you happen to be calling at the time you said you would in your P.S., and VITO did happen to pick up the phone, what you're saying here would remind VITO of the letter that came the other day.

That's a good thing.

Once VITO remembers that uniquely written, intriguing letter, VITO is likely to say something like this:

VITO: "This sounds familiar. Where did I read this? Did you send me a letter?"

You: "Yes, sure did. Mr. Benefito, what did you think of it?"

Or:

You: "Yes, Mr. Benefito, we suspect that similar or even greater results could happen at your organization between now and the end of this [calendar quarter]."

Even if VITO doesn't remember your correspondence, it's very possible that you will hear something like:

VITO: "How the heck did they do that in this economy?"

Give a *brief* (i.e., ten- to fifteen-second) answer to this question that spotlights your team (not you) and the benefits of doing business with your organization. Then . . .

If You Don't Get Interrupted, Here's What You'll Say Next

You: "Mr. Benefito, who on your team would you like me to continue this conversation with between now and the end of this business day?"

Or:

You: "Does this touch on issues that are of concern to you by the end of this [month, year, quarter]?"

Or:

You: "Are you interested in similar or even greater results by the end of this [year]?"

Or:

You: "Is this something that's consistent with what you're trying to achieve this [month, year, quarter]?"

Or:

You: "Would you favor [support/be interested in] such a solution for your business between now and the end of this [month]?"

Or:

You: "In your opinion, what is the best way for us to pursue this [issue/goal/conversation/idea]?"

That's it. That's all. Stop right there! This is your ending question.

At this point, there's no way that VITO will dismiss you or your offer! Yes, you may get some questions. Yes, you may get shunted to one or more of VITO's Decision Makers. All of these are outcomes that can lead you to another conversation with VITO—and get you one step closer to a permanent zip code in Sales Heaven!

Putting It All Together

Let's take a look at what you just did.

You started your telephone opening statement by saying VITO's name: "Mr. VITO Benefito?" Then you said a pleasantry: "It's an honor to speak with you." You paused for a quick moment, and continued with your Hook: "The [CEO] of the world's largest electronic manufacturer increased shareholder value and reduced cycle time by [63] days while eliminating [$87.9 million] in inventory, in just [144] days." Then, after you paused for a quick moment, you continued with an ending question: "Mr. Benefito, who on your team would you like me to continue this conversation with between now and the end of this business day?"

Right now you may be thinking, "Hey, wait a minute, Tony. I didn't get to say my name! And that 'ending question' would just get me sent to someone else and give VITO a chance to wiggle away from me!"

You're Right on Both Counts!

No, you didn't say your name. In fact, you made a point of *not* volunteering your name. (Although you did give it when you were asked directly.) And yes, you did set up a shunt to someone else at VITO, Inc. You did both of those things for a very good reason.

> » You didn't use your name in your opening statement because, until you're otherwise informed, VITO doesn't care what your name is! If VITO wants your name, you'll know.
> » You didn't ask VITO for anything other than a shunt to one of VITO's Decision Makers because *getting a shunt to a Decision Maker is an important outcome of this call.* I'll show you exactly what to do with that shunt a little later on in the book.

Now, let's look at some possible roadblocks and how to get around them.

Chapter 16

Three Obstacles, Eight Steps

In the last chapter, we put together our telephone opening statement, which means we're ready to deliver a meaningful (and easily interrupted) monologue to VITO. This is certainly a critical piece of our approach, but it's time for a reality check. Before we actually get to *deliver* that monologue, we may need to navigate three significant potential obstacles. They are:

1. A Receptionist Gatekeeper
2. One or more of VITO's personal assistants (very different from the Receptionist Gatekeeper, as we shall see)
3. The possibility of getting stymied by voice mail

With all of this in our way, it's no wonder we may hesitate just a little when it comes to prospecting for new business by making the dreaded cold call. I don't even like the *name* "cold call," do you?

Let's learn how to warm things up a bit.

Stairway to Sales Heaven

If you take the following eight steps, your calls will be put through to VITO. Period. What you're about to discover is a simple process. This process is going to take some work, but the rewards of having a conversation with VITO will be well worth the effort.

Step One: Create Your VITO Correspondence

You've already done this, right? (If not, go back and do it now.) Creating correspondence for VITO serves you in several important ways:

» First, it helps you create Equal Business Stature *before* you make your call.
» Second, it will make sure you navigate swiftly and sure footedly past the gatekeeper receptionist, as you'll see in a moment.
» Third, you will impress Tommie (VITO's personal assistant). That's certainly going to help your cause!
» Fourth, and perhaps most importantly, creating your correspondence will help you when it comes time to deliver your opening statement to VITO.

You can send your correspondence using the U.S. Postal Service first-class mail or any one of the many slick, professional-looking, inexpensive e-mail services. Here are some easy-to-follow guidelines.

Postal Format
Don't use your company logo at the top (or anywhere else) of the correspondence or envelope! Yeah, yeah, I know. Your logo is cool and you've been doing a lot of advertising lately and you're sponsor-

ing the regional champs in the local lacrosse tournament . . . but guess what? If you put it on your envelope and one of VITO's gatekeepers sees it, they will pass judgment as to what's inside. This is a bad thing. To avoid this outcome, you must promise *not* to use your company stationery or envelopes! Deal? Deal.

For a return address on the envelope, just put *your* name and address; don't put your company name. Don't worry, no one is going to send you anything anyway, and virtually no first-class mail gets lost these days!

By the way, don't write anything on the outside of the envelope like "Personal and Confidential" or "To be opened by addressee only."

Finally, use an 8½" × 11" or larger envelope for your letter. You want this correspondence to stand out. Use real postage stamps, too— not a postage meter. Please remember, because your VITO correspondence is in a large envelope, it will require some additional postage!

E-mail Format

Keep it simple! Keep it short!

If you're planning to e-mail the VITO correspondence that we created together a little while back, you'll have to edit it down. Everyone (including VITO) expects e-mail to be shorter than regular mail. Safety tip: Make sure you put your e-mail version through a spell checker before hitting send!

On many e-mail systems, what you create and see on your end may not be what VITO will see on his or her end. If you use any links, make sure they're tailored for *this* VITO. And make sure they work.

Stay away from catchy one-liners that aren't in your subject line, such as "Increased revenues and lower expenses with our new Zipline processors." The subject line should be a short version of your P.S. It could read like this:

Re: Our conversation on Thursday, May 14, at 9:30 A.M.

Step Two: Find Prospects in Your Territory That Match the Persona of Your Best Customers

You've already done this, too, right?

If you were able to answer yes honestly, then congratulations. You have identified a list of good solid prospects that are predisposed to buy from you! Send your VITO correspondence only to the organizations that fit that persona. Make sure you separate them into industries/niches.

Step Three: Find Out VITO's Name for Each of the Prospects in Step Two

This gets easier and easier to do with each passing day. There are tons of lists (some available for free, some for a small fee) that you can use. It's much easier to get VITO's name than most salespeople think.

Here's my general rule: If you really can't get your hands on VITO's name, if VITO is hiding behind a wall of secrecy, then you probably don't want that VITO as a customer.

Step Four: Find Out the Name of VITO's Personal Assistant

You'll need this for two very important reasons. First, to create your P.S. and that special handwritten message. Second, you'll need this name to interact effectively with the gatekeeper receptionist. Sometimes, you'll find these names on the same business list that VITO's name is on. Sometimes you won't.

"We created a 23% increase in shareholder economics while reaching full compliance in just 9 months for another CEO in your industry."

May 14, 2010

Mr. Benefito
President

Dear Mr. Benefito,

During the past seven years, we have worked with fifty-five organizations in the Computer manufacturing industry. We've listened, learned and created ideas and solutions. Collectively, we've been able to increase revenues and efficiencies while at the same time providing ways to increase shareholder value.

Are any of the following achievements on your list of goals, plans or objectives for the balance of this calendar year? If so, the good news is that now we're ready to offer these ideas for your consideration.

- **Increased revenues** of up to 44% per year have been reported by our clients.
- **Effectiveness and Efficiency enhancements** increased production of finished goods to 15%.
- **Fully Protect Market Share** eliminate the need to 'win-back' existing customers while increasing brand recognition and awareness.
- **Greater Add-on Business** capture higher-margin, add-on business by as much as 120% annually!

Mr. Benefito, it's obvious you know your organization better than anyone does. But, what may not be so obvious is how we could help you realize similar or even greater results before the end of this calendar year. If you would like to take the first step, our complete team of experts can quickly determine each and every possibility.

To greater success,

SAMPLE

Wil Prosper
760-603-0017

P.S. I will call your office on Thursday, May 18 at 10:00 AM. If this is not the best time for our first conversation, please have Tommie call me to reschedule the call.

The fastest and most accurate way to discover VITO's personal assistant's name? Call VITO, Inc. and ask!

Step Five: Find Out VITO, Inc's Fax Number

Why do you need this? Because you'll be *faxing* your VITO correspondence to VITO, Inc. one hour before your call to VITO! And, on that *faxed* copy of the correspondence, you will:

» Circle the headline and write above, below, or along the side: *Is this important to you and your operation in the next [90 days]?*
» Circle or draw an arrow to one or more of the benefit bullets: *Are these results on your list of to-dos this [month]?*
» Underline the time of your call in the P.S.: *Looking forward to our first conversation!*

Step Six: Find the Name(s) of Each of the Decision Makers Who Represent Your Perfect "Shunt" Target

Which Decision Maker(s) are most likely to be empowered by VITO to take a closer look into your ideas? For example, in my case, that's the VP of Sales or the CPO (Chief Performance Officer) or CMO (Chief Marketing Officer).

Why do you need to know about any of this? Well, if at any point in time anyone (including VITO) suggests a shunt to anyone other than your ideal shunt target, you can immediately stop the shunt in its tracks! (That skill, by the way, is critically important to controlling your sales process and the size of your commission checks!)

We'll discuss shunts in more depth in a later chapter.

Step Seven: Internalize Your Telephone Opening Statement

I didn't say memorize it; I said internalize it.

If you memorize it, it will sound like you're reading it from a script. When you internalize an opening statement, you'll never say it the same way twice. "Filler" words ("uh," "um," "you know") are okay in moderation. We're looking for a casual, relaxed, and much-less-than-perfect delivery.

Step Eight: Prepare Your Voice Mail Message to VITO

Yes, I know that you've been struggling with voice mail jail. I also know that no one's been returning your calls. All of that is about to change, as you'll see in Chapter 18.

VITO RULE #22 Once you complete all eight of the precorrespondence steps, and not before, you will be ready to send your VITO correspondence.

I strongly recommend that your first wave of VITO letters be sent out to at least twenty VITOs. Keep reading to find out how you will follow through on these steps.

Chapter 17

The Gatekeepers

The first Gatekeeper you'll encounter, the Receptionist Gatekeeper is *not* VITO's Personal Assistant, but someone who fields calls for a living, typically at the front desk. Receptionist Gatekeepers handle a lot of phone traffic. Given the advent of "press star-1 to hear a directory" technology on most of our business phone systems, and the rise of e-mail and texting as business communications media, with every passing year there are fewer receptionists sitting in lobbies answering phones and opening snail mail. Even so, all it takes is one receptionist to stop you dead in your tracks.

Before you pick up the phone to call VITO, you must master a few simple facts about Receptionist Gatekeepers. Namely:

- » They are not the highest-paid employees at VITO, Inc.
- » Their job is to be polite and route calls as quickly and accurately as possible to the appropriate individuals at VITO, Inc.
- » They are trained to protect the time of key individuals; that means they are trained to pick up on any uncertainty in your voice or what you're saying.
- » They can smell an unsolicited sales call a mile away.

How do you deal with these folks? Let's make a VITO call and hear what an ideal interaction with a Receptionist Gatekeeper sounds like.

It's V-Day!

You did all the research. You selected twenty VITOs who match the persona of your best customers (if you don't have any customers yet, then match the persona of your ideal prospects). You got the names (and pronunciations) for both VITO and Tommie. You sent your VITO letter a few days ago, and you *faxed* it exactly one hour before your scheduled time to call. Now it's V-Day—VITO Day—two minutes before the time you promised VITO and Tommie, in your P.S., that you would call.

You start punching VITO, Inc.'s number. The reason you're calling two minutes early is simple: Being "on time" for VITO calls (as opposed to any other kind of call) means you should be a little bit early!

The phone rings. Here's what happens next.

Receptionist Gatekeeper: VITO, Inc., how may I direct your call?

You: Please connect me with [Tommie] in [Ms. Importanta's] office, this is [Will, Will Prosper]. Thank you!

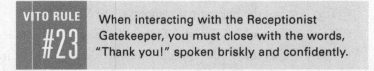

VITO RULE #23 — When interacting with the Receptionist Gatekeeper, you must close with the words, "Thank you!" spoken briskly and confidently.

Notice that, in this critical first exchange with the Receptionist Gatekeeper, you're giving three critical bits of information in a specific (and quite intentional) order:

First, you're sharing Tommie's name. Here's the reason: The Receptionist Gatekeeper knows that Tommie plays a bigger game on a bigger field at VITO, Inc., and is really the first line of defense when it comes to VITO and protecting VITO's precious time.

Second, you're sharing VITO's name. Here's the reason: Saying VITO's name confidently makes it clear that you know what's going on. You're signaling to the Receptionist Gatekeeper that you're well informed, that you know who's who, and that's important.

Third, you're sharing your own name. Here's the reason: The Receptionist Gatekeeper will ask for it anyway.

You must give these pieces of information, in this order. The bottom line is this: If you follow this sequence, you're actually doing the Receptionist Gatekeeper's job for him or her!

Now, let's assume that the Receptionist Gatekeeper says this:

Receptionist Gatekeeper: What's the call about?

You've got two choices when it comes to formulating a response here.

Response 1

You: "[Ms. Importanta] is expecting my call at [9:30]. Would you please put me through? Thank you!"

Repeat: *You must close with the words, "Thank you!" spoken briskly and confidently!*

Response 2

You: "My call to [Ms. Importanta] is about [increasing shareholder value, reducing cycle time and eliminating $87.9 million in inventory]. Now, it appears that I am running a bit late for my call. Would you please connect me to Tommie? Thank you!"

And once again: *You must close with the words, "Thank you!" spoken briskly and confidently!*

Assuming that you are thinking, breathing, and speaking while channeling your own inner VITO, you will find that this approach will virtually always get your call put through without further interrogation. *If you sound like VITO, you will be forwarded to VITO's office!*

By the way, if what I am advocating seems forceful, controlling, or manipulative (three words I hear at about this point in the program), I suggest that you take a moment to stop and think about what *your* organization's VITO would sound like if he or she were interacting with a Receptionist Gatekeeper and wanting to be connected.

What's Next?

You're about to enter VITO's private suite. Next, we'll consider what you'll say to Tommie, VITO's trusted personal assistant. These are two *totally different* players at VITO, Inc., and the sooner you recognize that, the better off (and bigger) your commission check will be!

VITO's Personal Assistant, Tommie

Good news! The closer you get to VITO, the easier the process gets. Once the Receptionist Gatekeeper puts your call through to Tommie's office, one of these three things will take place:

1. Tommie will answer the phone
2. Voice mail will answer the phone
3. VITO will answer the phone

I'll cover the first of these options in this chapter. The next chapter will cover what you do if you hit voice mail. And the chapter after that will give you more ammunition for the moment you finally hit pay dirt and make voice-to-voice contact with VITO.

Tommie Picks Up the Phone

You hear one ring, two rings, and then . . .

Tommie: "Good Morning, Ms. Importanta's office, this is Tommie."

Tommie holds the key to winning VITO's precious time and attention, either directly (as in, you get to talk to VITO) or indirectly (as in, Tommie talks favorably to VITO about you). In recognition of that critical fact, I want you to take the following critically important step the moment you hear Tommie's voice:

VITO RULE #24	When talking with Tommie, forget that VITO exists!

That's right. For all intents and purposes, VITO just left the planet! That's why I want you to say your opening statement to Tommie . . . with *one small exception* and *one small addition*.

The exception is pretty obvious: You'll be using Tommie's name instead of VITO's. The addition is that, with Tommie, you *will* be using your name and your company name. (Tommie will need to know this to make a mental connection with you and your letter). What you say might sound something like this:

You: "Tommie, thanks for taking my call! This is [Will, Will Prosper, with ZipLine]. The [CEO] of the world's largest electronic manufacturer increased shareholder value and reduced cycle time by

[63] days while eliminating $87.9 million in inventory, in just [144] days. Does this touch on issues that are of concern to you during this [month, year, quarter]?"

Notice that you are *not mentioning VITO!*

Notice that you are *treating Tommie as though Tommie WERE VITO!*

Here's What Will Happen Next

Tommie will make a mental connection about you, your letter, its headline, and your opening statement's hook, and shortly after doing that will probably answer your question with something that sounds like this:

Tommie: "Shareholder value, reducing time to market, and cutting expenses is always important to Ms. Importanta."

Look at what just happened. You asked if something was important to Tommie, and Tommie replied with what is important to VITO. I have heard this happen hundreds of times. No, make that *thousands* of times.

But guess what? If you make the common mistake of asking Tommie what *VITO* thinks (even though you are supposed to be operating under the assumption that VITO has left the planet), this is what your conversational sequence will look like:

You: "Does this touch on issues that are of concern to Ms. Importanta during this [month, year, quarter]?"

Tommie: "Send me some information on what this is all about and if Ms. Importanta is interested she'll give you a call."

You can pull out your bugle and play "Taps" for yourself at this point, because you just threw yourself under the bus. You ignored Tommie's valuable insights and neglected to salute Tommie's uniform!

General Rules of Engagement with Tommie

Follow these rules of engagement in your everyday interactions with Tommie, and you'll be rewarded with invaluable insights into VITO, Inc.—and get the access to VITO's world that less fortunate sales-people only dream of.

- » **Do Not** ask to speak to VITO. This will have the effect of dismissing Tommie.
- » **Do Not** ask whether VITO is in; Tommie will automatically say no.
- » **Do Not** ask whether VITO got your letter; this request has the look and feel of Tommie working for you, and that's not good either.
- » **Do Not** lie to Tommie about anything.
- » **Do Not** say you know someone when you don't.
- » **Do Not** sidestep any question.
- » **Do Not** dig for information without giving information.
- » **Do Not** overstate or inflate anything (like who your customers are, how many you have, and what results you've been delivering).
- » **Do Not** pass along any outdated, misleading, or inaccurate information.
- » **Do** pronounce VITO and Tommie's names correctly. If you have to make a couple of calls beforehand to ask someone else at VITO, Inc. about the correct pronunciations, do so.
- » **Do** follow Tommie's advice and guidance.
- » **Do** listen carefully and take notes.
- » **Do** answer every question Tommie asks.
- » **Do** give information before you ask for it.
- » **Do** ask very specific questions.

» **Do** follow up with a handwritten thank-you note *immediately* after your first conversation with Tommie. You can also send an e-mail, as long as you *also* send a nice handwritten note via snail mail.

During the call, Tommie, like VITO, may try to point you toward someone specific at VITO, Inc. As I hope you remember, this is called a shunt. There are good shunts and bad shunts; I'll show you how to tell the difference and turn a bad one into a good one in a later chapter.

Chapter 18

Voice Mail Messages

Okay. VITO isn't in; Tommie isn't in; you get dumped into VITO's voice mail. What do you do?

Before I answer that question, let me ask *you*: What has your experience been with leaving voice mail messages? In other words, how high is leaving voice mail messages on your list of things you'd like to be doing as part of your sales work?

If you're like the majority of salespeople I work with, your interactions with voice mail have probably left you thinking about going back to school to get a degree in finance, or maybe something *really* interesting, like parks and recreation services. You've probably asked yourself, at one time or another, "What's the use of leaving a voice mail message? Nothing ever seems to come of it."

Well, all of that is about to change. Right now.

Voice mail is actually a great and underused sales tool. *Most of the people and organizations you're competing against are not using it effectively.* You're going to begin taking advantage of that fact!

The *right* voice mail message will quickly put you on the radar screen of VITO, Tommie, or both. In many situations, the voice mail message you leave for VITO will be forwarded on to one or more of VITO's trusted Decision Makers.

Delivery of Your Voice Mail Message

You may not be able to control what happens *to* your message, but you certainly can control what happens *during* your message! We've already covered how important it is to deliver a Balanced Gain Equation, which is music to VITO's ears. Now, for your voice mail message, the vocal delivery is *by far* the most important factor in getting a return call.

VITO RULE #25 The tone, modulation, and pacing of your voice will determine how easy or difficult it is for VITO to listen to (and act on!) your message.

The best tone to use in your voice mail to VITO is your natural one—and the fastest way to know what your natural tone is will be to pick up your phone right now and call your own voice mail system. Once you hear the beep, hum your favorite song and let your system record it. (Yes, you may want to do this while no one else is around).

Have you done that? Good. Don't call your message box yet. Keep reading.

After you develop the text you'll be using for your first message to VITO (that will be in just a minute), I want you to use that text to leave a *second* voice mail message for yourself.

When you listen to *both* of these messages (which should be after you've finished reading this chapter), I want you to ask yourself a question: Is your "hum" the same basic pitch and tone as your voice was while you were reading your message? If it is, congratulations, you're using your natural tone! If it isn't, you need to practice by humming a bar of that favorite song and then speaking a bar. Do this until your hum and your spoken words come out the same. (This, too, is something you may want to do while no one else is around.)

The modulation of your voice should vary and be in concert with the message you're delivering. You do this by changing your voice in accordance with the words and phrases you'll be using. You'll want to raise the pitch of your voice during the last few words of any question you ask and lower the pitch of your voice during the last few words of any statement you're making. The best advice I can give you on this score is to tune in to your favorite news anchor and close your eyes as you listen. You'll be able to hear what I mean.

The volume of your voice should remain constant throughout your entire voice mail message.

Pacing refers to the speed of your spoken word. Since VITOs are fast-paced individuals, it's best to deliver your voice mail message with a *slightly* faster pace than you would normally speak in person or over the telephone. Of course, your message must always be comprehensible.

In addition to implementing the advice I've just shared with you, you should follow these simple guidelines:

Be authentic

Don't sound like you're reading from a script. Just as we discussed with your opening statement during voice-to-voice contact, you'll internalize your messages, not memorize your messages!

Deliver your message with enthusiasm

You must sound believable. Therefore, you must truly believe that what you have to say is music to VITO's ears. Remember, you and

VITO have much in common. Personality-wise you're almost twins! People who have similar outlooks and interests like to look out for each other and keep each other in the loop when they come across something interesting and exciting. That's exactly what you're going to be doing with VITO when you leave this message. What you have to say will be well received if you're sincerely excited about it. Once you're excited about it, VITO will be excited too!

Follow up appropriately once you leave a voice mail message
Don't expect to leave just one message and get a call back immediately from VITO (although that, too, will happen); set up a plan. You must (and will) be prepared to leave a series of messages. Build this follow-through plan into whatever calendar or scheduling system you're using now.

Every voice mail message you leave must be different
Each message must set up the next message, and the next part of the story line.

Voice Mail Message Number One

Your first message is going to be your opening statement that you would have said to VITO if VITO had been in to take your call, amplified with what I call "bookends" at the beginning and end. Take a look at the script below, and notice how I've added the bookends (which are *italicized*) before and after the opening statement:

You: "[Mr. Benefito], this is [Will, Will Prosper] with [ZipLine]— *if you were in your office to take my call, this is what you would have heard:* The [CEO] of the world's largest electronic manufacturer increased shareholder value and reduced cycle time by [63] days while eliminating [$87.9 million in inventory], in just [144] days. *This topic could be important to both of us. That's why you'll be hearing from me again [today] at [1:30], or if you like, you can call me before then at [800-877-8486]. Have a masterful rest of the day!"*

You can also modify the closing bookend and say something like this:

You: "This topic could be important to both of us, that's why you'll be hearing from me [one week from today] on [Tuesday, May 24, at 2:30 P.M.], or, if you like, you can call me before then at [800-877-8486] anytime after [4:00 P.M.]. Until then, have a prosperous rest of the week!"

VITO Voice Mail Message Number Two

Of course, you'll make an attempt to connect with VITO at exactly the time you said you would at the end of your last voice mail message. If VITO isn't in to take your call, you must be prepared to continue with your story line. Your second message could sound something like this:

"[Ms. Importanta], [Will Prosper] here. Since you listened to my last voice mail message, we've created two additional results with that top [manufacturer]: [Full compliance with government regulations] and [risk mitigation for wrongful termination litigation's]. If you like, we can get into the details as early as [tomorrow at 1:30 P.M.], or, if you like, you can reach me at [800-877-8486]. Thanks for your continued interest, and have a great rest of the day."

Note that we've added some new information. That's critical to getting a call back from VITO or Tommie or someone else, like one of VITO's key Decision Makers.

VITO Voice Mail Message Number Three

You'll recall one of the most important methods and mindsets of VITOs is that they love to win and hate to lose. In your third voice mail message, you'll begin to introduce the probability of an underlying consequence and subsequent possibility of loss that may result from not taking action on the value you have to offer VITO, Inc.

You: "[Ms. Importanta], [Will Prosper] here. As we move into the [last quarter] of this [calendar year], [three] of our key [manufacturing] customers are posting up to [$80,000.00] per month cost cutting with [no] increase in [capital expense]. [Ms. Importanta], we suspect the possibility of unintentional inefficiencies taking place in your [manufacturing] operation that we could stop within the next [45 days]. All it will take to answer that question is a call back from you or the person you hold most responsible for your [manufacturing] operation. You can reach me at [800-777-8486] between [now and the end of this business day]. If not, I'll reach out to you on [Friday], [June 4], at [4:30 P.M.] Thanks for listening to this rather long voice mail message!"

Of course, the numbers you use must be realistic. Notice here that I use the words "unintentional," "suspect," and "possibility." These phrases soften the message and make it more credible.

VITO Voice Mail Message Number Four

It's been my personal experience that by the time you get to your fourth message, someone will either call you back and tell you to stop calling—or engage with you.

True story: Moments after leaving my fourth voice mail message for the president of one of the largest office supply companies in North America, my phone rang. What I heard took me by surprise:

"You've been leaving voice mail messages for my president and she's been forwarding them to me with her own comments." (You'll notice here that the caller didn't identify himself, or his company name, or give me VITO's name.) I said, "Oh, that's interesting. What was her comment about my last voice mail message?" The response was music to my ears: "She said to find out what it would take to have you teach our salespeople to leave messages like the ones you've been leaving for her!"

I was hired to give a keynote speech in Las Vegas for 1,600 eager salespeople. My cost of sale: four voice mail messages. I love this stuff!

In your fourth voice mail message to VITO, you'll subtly introduce a personal concern that maybe something has run amuck with VITO's communications infrastructure. It sounds like this:

You: "[Ms. Importanta], this is [Will Prosper], just realizing that perhaps you have not received my last three voice mail messages, so I've taken the time to fax you the original correspondence that we sent along with some other interesting information about our proven ideas for the [manufacturing industry]. The question becomes, can our team of industry experts achieve similar or even greater results for your enterprise? Your return call to me will begin to answer that question. In the meantime, please consider this: Our customers look at our relationship as an appreciating asset, which continues to pay dividends long after they decide to become one of our valued customers. If you would like, return my call [today between the hours of 1:00 and 3:00 P.M. Eastern time] at [800-777-8486] or, if it's okay with you, I'll reach out and make another attempt to contact you at [11:45 A.M.] today. Thanks for listening to this voice mail message!"

Aren't you glad you took the time to get VITO's fax number? (By the way, you can also use VITO's e-mail address for this same purpose.)

At this point, you can start the process all over again from start to finish if you want.

Chapter 19

Pay Dirt

Pay dirt (n): Any source of success or wealth; a fortunate discovery or profitable venture—*dictionary.com*

Okay, you're ready! You sent your letter to VITO. It's exactly the time you said you would call VITO. You've got some butterflies in your stomach. You know what? That's good. You need some energy and some excitement for this call. You use it to pick up that 3,000-pound phone and dial VITO's number.

You do and . . . VITO picks up!

You lay your opening statement out, exactly as I've taught you. At this point, there are six things that can happen—all of them good.

VITO RULE #26 Be ready for each of the six good things that can happen during a call to VITO.

Good Thing Number One

VITO interrupts you (remember, that's a good thing) and your conversation goes like this:

VITO: "Hold on. I don't have time for this. I am heading off to a meeting (or whatever other emergency is currently playing out at VITO, Inc.)."

You: "Okay. When we do have a chance to catch up, let's make sure we chat about increasing your [shareholder value] while [cutting your time to market] and saving up to [$87,000] in [monthly] [inventory costs]."

Now comes the hard part. *Stop talking.* Pause . . . and wait and see what happens next.

Here's what could happen. That meeting that VITO was running off to will be put on hold and you'll hear something like this:

VITO: "And exactly how do you do that?"

You: "Well, which part should we look at first—[increasing shareholder value], [cutting time to market], or [slashing inventory costs]?"

Good Thing Number Two

You lay out your opening statement, and VITO interrupts you and says:

VITO: "This doesn't sound like anything I'd be interested in."

You: "Okay, no surprise. Before you get back to your busy day, let me ask you: In what area of your organization do you want to see the biggest improvements in the shortest amounts of time?"

Now comes the hard part. *Stop talking.* Pause . . . and see what happens next.

Here's what could happen.

VITO: "Since you ask—manufacturing cost over-runs."

You: "We have a [proven process] that typically involves [three specific areas] they are: [Yap, Yap, and Yap]. Which one would you like to dive into right now?"

> **Caution:** What you definitely *do not* want to do is a *feature* dump on VITO! Make sure what you say is rich in benefits and hard and soft value.

Good Thing Number Three

VITO interrupts you and says:

VITO: "No thanks. We've got all the help we need in this area. Our current business relationships are satisfying our needs."

You: "Ms. Importanta, would you like to know if your loyalty to your existing source of supply could be costing you anything?"

Now comes the hard part. *Stop talking*. Pause . . . and wait and see what happens next.

Here's what could happen.

VITO: "What do you mean by that?"

You: "Of the [756] customers we have, [34] are in your industry, and we've been able to [increase shareholder value], [cut time to market], and save over [$87,000] each [month] of [inventory costs]. Is this substantial enough for us to dive a bit deeper into what results we suspect we can deliver to your organization in the next [90 days]?"

Good Thing Number Four

VITO interrupts you and says:

VITO: "Why don't you just send me some information?"

You: (Because you don't yet know whether this VITO prefers to learn by watching, listening, or reading) "Great idea. Would you prefer to watch, listen, or read about how we've been able to [increase shareholder value], [cut time to market], and save over [$87,000] each [month] of [inventory costs] for [34] other [CEOs] in the [manufacturing industry]?"

Now comes the hard part. *Stop talking*. Pause . . . and wait and see what happens next.

Here's what could happen.

VITO: "Tell me the short version right now."

You: "Okay. Which of the three areas would you like to dive into right now: [increased shareholder value], [reduced time to market], or [reduced costs]?"

> **Caution:** What you definitely *do not* want to do is a *feature* dump on VITO! Make sure what you say is rich in benefits and hard and soft value.

Good Thing Number Five

VITO interrupts you and says:

VITO: "We're too busy for this right now. Why don't you call me back in six months?"

You: "Okay. Just to let you know, though, there's a strong possibility that during that time your organization could unintentionally waste as much as [$260,000] of your hard-earned revenue."

Now comes the hard part. *Stop talking*. Pause . . . wait and see what happens.

Here's what could happen.

VITO: "Where the heck did you come up with that number?"

You: "We've saved [34] other [CEOs] that much revenue and we strongly suspect that we can deliver similar or even greater results with your [manufacturing operations] in the next [90 days]."

Good Thing Number Six

VITO tries to point you toward someone else at VITO, Inc. Congratulations! This is exactly what you wanted to happen. I'll show you how to handle this best-case scenario in the next chapter.

Remember, getting shunted is one of your major desired outcomes here. You're not trying to close this deal over the phone. You want to qualify this opportunity and earn an appointment if possible and, eventually, earn what I call a *golden referral*. I'll show you how to do both, as soon as I share one more nugget with you about these critical opening seconds of this first call.

THE LAST WORD ABOUT PAY DIRT

Pay dirt is not any one deal; it's your peer-to-peer relationship with VITO. If you stand your ground, know when to talk, and know when to stop talking, as I've taught you in this chapter, that relationship will be there for you whenever you need it as your sales process moves forward at VITO, Inc.

Chapter 20

Dealing with the Shunt; Qualifying the Opportunity

When it comes to dealing with shunts at this stage of the process, there are really only two varieties: those that come from Tommie and those that come from VITO. In handling both, remember a principle I've shared with you earlier. It's one of the most important of all the VITO rules, and it amounts to a *Golden Rule of Shunts*.

 VITO RULE #27 You will inevitably be shunted to the person within VITO, Inc. whom you sound the most like.

In other words, if you want to begin your sales cycle with Seemore (and I know you don't), then go ahead and sound like Seemore. If you want to begin your sales cycle with VITO, then you'd better sound like VITO. With that important principle in mind, let's look at the two worlds where you are likely to encounter shunts: Tommie's world and VITO's world.

Tommie's World

The easiest way for VITO's Personal Assistant to dust off a salesperson is to shunt him or her to someone of lesser authority. Here's what might happen. Shortly before the time you are supposed to call VITO, your inbound line rings. You pick up the receiver and a crisp, professional-sounding voice says:

Tommie: "Mr. Prosper, this is Tommie, from Mr. Benefito's office, calling to tell you that Mr. Benefito looked at your letter and wants you to contact our purchasing department. Friday is the day our buyers accept calls from companies that start with a 'Z.' Have a nice day, I've got to run to catch another line."

If *this* happens to you, it's because you didn't take me up on my offer to help you create your VITO correspondence—*For Free*! You followed the path of least resistance, and did it yourself. Too bad! But it's not too late. After you complete this chapter, turn to page 229 of this book and follow the instructions. You'll be on the fast track to Sales Heaven, where you'll never, ever have to deal with this kind of demoralizing inbound call!

Alternatively, you're making your very first call to VITO, at precisely the right day and time. You call VITO's line and hear one ring, two rings, three rings, and then:

Tommie: "Ms. Importanta's office, this is Tommie. How may I help you?"

You: "Tommie, thanks for taking my call! This is [Will, Will Prosper, with ZipLine]. The [CEO] of the world's largest electronic manufacturer . . .

Tommie interrupts you with:

Tommie: "Just a second, Mr. Prosper. I've got your letter right here. It would be best if you contacted our chief operations officer; she's in charge of all infrastructure resources, including our manufacturing operations. Hold on; let me connect you."

What do you do?

You'll recall that, a little earlier in the book, I suggested that you know the names and titles of the Decision Maker(s) who would serve your sales efforts best; in my case, as someone who helps sales teams, that's typically the VP of Sales or CMO (Chief Marketing Officer). Who is it in your case? Who would VITO hold most responsible for implementing the results of whatever it is you sell? If you don't know, you're not ready to deal with shunts from *either* Tommie's world *or* VITO's world.

Take a minute and write the title(s) here. Don't go any further with this program until you've filled in the relevant titles that are the perfect shunt target for what you sell!

Turn the page when you're done.

If you wrote down any title lower than a Decision Maker, go back to Chapter 1, and start reading this book all over again!

Still with me? Great. Now, knowing the right title isn't enough. You'll also need to know the *names* of the individuals who match up with the titles. Yes, you must do this for each of the organizations you make your VITO launch on. Assuming, that is, that you want to effectively sidestep any premature shunts and make sure the shunts you *do* get are the shunts you want.

Let's take that first situation, where Tommie called you and wants to shunt you to the bowels of VITO, Inc.

Tommie: ". . . Mr. Benefito looked at your letter and wants you to contact our purchasing department."

I hope you know by now that if you let this shunt to the bottom of the organization's totem-pole happen, you'll spiral into a long, drawn-out sales cycle that will be paved with lots to do and end with little or no business and a one-way ticket to Linoleumville.

Here's how to stop this shunt to Sales Hell.

You: "Tommie, thanks, but your purchasing department may not be the best place for us to start our process of understanding exactly how we can, in the next [144] days, increase shareholder value, reduce cycle time, and eliminate as much as $87.9 million in monthly inventory costs."

Pause *briefly,* and then continue with:

You: "Another major [manufacturer] found that their COO was able to quickly evaluate our ideas. In your organization, that would be [Justin Tyme]."

IMPORTANT NOTE: If you don't know the name of the Decision Maker of choice at VITO, Inc., this response will lose much of its power!

Pause *briefly,* and continue with:

You: "Would you like to introduce me to [Justin Tyme] or would you prefer that I make the call on my own?"

No matter what answer you get, you're going to want to *qualify* this lead before you reach out to Justin and say that Tommie, in VITO's office, sent you. I'll be sharing more with you about qualifying in just a second. First, though, let's look at the next situation, where Tommie wants to prematurely shunt you to a Decision Maker who definitely *isn't* the person you want to talk to.

Tommie: "Just a second, Mr. Prosper. I've got your letter right here. It would be best if you contacted our chief operations officer. He's in charge of all infrastructure resources, including our manufacturing operations. Hold on; let me connect you."

Now, I realize you will be sorely tempted to take this shunt. After all, the COO of any organization isn't a bad place to start your sales process. There are, however, a few questions you still need to ask Tommie in order to fully *qualify* this opportunity.

1. What specific goals, plans, and objectives must be overachieved over the next month (or quarter, or other specific period of time) at VITO, Inc.?
2. What are the expectations of a business partner that can help accomplish that for VITO, Inc.?
3. If the objectives in Number 1 and the expectations in Number 2 can be exceeded, would VITO consider you his or her business partner of choice during the next month (or quarter, or other specific period of time)?

Yes, you *must* ask Tommie these questions, and get clear answers, before accepting this shunt. And remember, you are interacting with Tommie *as though VITO did not exist*. If you do that, then you will find, more often than not, that Tommie will share (or track down) VITO's benchmarks in all these areas.

Do not accept a shunt from an unqualified opportunity!

VITO's World

You begin your first call with VITO, and because it's your lucky day, VITO interrupts you with a proposed shunt.

VITO: "Hold on. I remember seeing this somewhere. It would be best if you contacted our chief operations officer. He's in charge of all infrastructure resources, including our manufacturing operations. Hold on; let me get Tommie to connect you."

You: "Mr. Benefito, before your COO [Justin Tyme] spends his valuable time with me, let me ask you something. What expectations do you have of a [business partner or provider] that can help you overachieve your goals of [increasing shareholder value], [further reduce your cycle time], and [cut monthly inventory costs]?"

By the way, if you sent your letter, and your opening statement was tagged into your headline, and VITO was interested enough to shunt you to a Decision Maker, you basically know the answer to Question Number 1 above. Ask the question anyway. After you get your answer, move on to:

You: "If [Justin] confirms that your objectives in this area can be exceeded by working with us, and if we meet your expectations for a business partner, can you see our company becoming VITO, Inc.'s business partner of choice during [the next fiscal year]?"

I realize that you're probably not used to qualifying an opportunity in this way, and I realize, too, that you've probably been given a lot of advice about other ways to qualify opportunities. (This advice typically involves spending a lot of time with Seemore.) I want you to *change your process* and *ask VITO this question directly while you have VITO on the line!*

Would you like to know *why* it's so important for you to ask VITO (and or Tommie) this kind of question? It's simple: *VITO and Tommie are the only people in the enterprise who both a) know the answer and b) are willing to share that answer with you on the first call!*

If VITO says, "Yes," salute and follow VITO's orders!

If VITO says, "No," ask this question:

You: "Mr. Benefito, you most likely have a good reason for saying that; could you please tell me what it is?"

Qualified or Unqualified?

If VITO and or Tommie tells you frankly there is *no daylight*, as in *no chance to win business this fiscal year* (or whatever other timeframe you asked about), say, "Thank you," and make a note to check back again in three months or so. Do not invest your time, effort, and energy in this opportunity. You have not qualified it.

If VITO and or Tommie tells you that you *have a shot* (and you are much more likely to get this information than you think), accept the shunt. Follow the breadcrumbs to the Decision Maker's door.

Remember these three questions?

1. What specific goals, plans, and objectives must be overachieved over the next month (or quarter or other specific period of time) at VITO, Inc.?
2. What are the expectations of a business partner that can help accomplish that for VITO, Inc.?
3. If the objectives in Number 1 and the expectations in Number 2 can be exceeded, would VITO consider you his or her business partner of choice during the next month (or quarter or other specific period of time)?

You must—I repeat, must—get these answers from either VITO or Tommie (preferably VITO) before you proceed to go anywhere else in VITO, Inc.

VITO RULE #28

Do not accept shunts from unqualified opportunities!

Ask yourself: Would *your* organization's VITO accept a shunt without determining the benchmarks for success on both sides of the relationship?

Assuming you are able to confirm that you *do* have a shot (and if you've created a good target personal list, the odds are quite good that you do), you now face an important question. How do you make sure that your *first* contact with VITO's corner office isn't your *last* contact?

I'll answer that little brain teaser for you in our next chapter.

Chapter 21

Second Contact

Getting the second appointment with VITO is a lot like dating. Whatever happens (or doesn't) before, during, and after your first date is going to have a serious impact on your chances for getting the second date! What you're about to learn will up your chances of getting that all-important "second date" with VITO.

Whenever you read the word "appointment" in this chapter, understand that I mean either a telephone or in-person appointment. You may be one of those salespeople who do virtually all of your selling over the phone or through other virtual communications media (like Skype); if that's the case, you'll find that the tactics I share with you here can be adapted very easily to your world.

Some words of warning: If you've been reading all the material in this book but not actually doing any of the activities, I'm afraid what follows won't be of much help to you. Ditto if you have already stumbled upon VITO by some method other than the ones I've shared with you, and are now looking for a quick fix that will get you back on VITO's radar screen. To get the entire program to work, you've got to work the entire program!

Before You Reach Out to VITO for the Very First Time

I am assuming that you . . .

1. Know VITO's industry
2. Know what hard dollar value and soft dollar value you can deliver
3. Know how you've delivered it to others in VITO's industry
4. Know or suspect what the value to this VITO might be
5. Know how to articulate Numbers 1, 2, 3, and 4 above in a way that VITO can easily understand

All of what I've shared with you thus far has been designed to put you in the position of nodding your head and saying, "Check!" as you read the list above. And by, "Check!" I don't mean, "Yes, it would be a good idea for me to know that," but rather, "Yes, I actually do know this about one or more specific VITOs in my territory." If you're missing one or more items on the "check" list, *you are not yet ready for this chapter.* Go back and fill in the blanks, and then come back, so you can take advantage of what you'll find here.

Once you're up to speed on all that, it becomes your responsibility to use the Internet, your own organization's marketing materials and research, and your own contacts to figure out your own best-guess answers to the following three questions:

1. What are the three biggest challenges *this* VITO's industry is facing? (If you can snag a real or virtual copy of the trade magazine that covers your target VITO's industry, you'll have the answer to this in about five minutes.)

2. Who is currently working with companies like VITO, Inc. to address these challenges/opportunities? (Check out the ads in that trade magazine. Most likely, it's someone you compete with. Go to that company's website and look at their customer success stories and testimonials.)

3. How do you stack up against those outfits? (Point for point, what are the major differences between you and your competition? How do those differences impact the industry that this VITO is in? What do you have that your competition doesn't have that may be important to this VITO?)

If you've got good answers to all of the above questions, you're well positioned to set up a second appointment with VITO. If you don't, you're not.

What Do You Want?

Whether you hear it out loud or not, VITO will almost certainly want to know the answer to this question: "What do you want?"

Before reaching out to VITO, set yourself up for the second appointment by asking yourself these questions:

» What do I want as an outcome of this appointment?
» What would VITO want as an outcome of this appointment?
» What's the best mutual outcome of this appointment for both VITO and me?
» In the last sale I made that was larger than my average sale AND that closed in less time than my average sale, what took place immediately after my first appointment?

When the answers to all four of these questions line up, guess what? You've got a good possible outcome to your first appointment and a good reason for your second appointment.

By the way, that last question is critical. On the last sale you closed that was higher than average in value and faster than average in closing, *what did you do?* Did you ask for and receive any specific information that was critical for you to put together a proposal? Did you do a demo or presentation of any kind? Whatever you did, is it possible you could do it again, with this VITO?

VITO RULE #29

Know what you want from the meeting.

The Must-Do List for Your First Appointment

What follows is a non-negotiable must-do list for your first telephone *or* in-person contact with VITO. Sure, there will be other activities and ingredients, but omitting or glossing over any one of these items will dramatically lessen your chances of getting the second appointment.

Must-do *items that apply to both telephone and in-person contacts:*

Be specific. VITO divides salespeople into two groups: those who use "weasel words" and those who don't. Be sure to land in the right group.

Speak with VITO; never talk to VITO. Speaking means that you have VITO's purpose and results in mind.

Give VITO choices. As in, "Would you like to discuss four proven ideas to increase margins over the next 120 days or is there something else that's more important to you by the end of [May]?"

Follow VITO's lead. Don't try to take over the meeting or impose your agenda. Be prepared to shift course and dig deeper when you hear VITO say things like:

> » "We have more important issues to be concerned about."
> » "We'll take a look at what you're offering after the second quarter."
> » "What would you be able to do if we . . . ?"
> » "Is it possible to . . . ?"
> » "How could we . . . ?"

No "F" words. Stay away from Features, Functions, or Facts that are of no interest to VITO. Remember, you will be shunted to the person whom you sound most like.

No long, drawn-out monologues. If VITO isn't participating in a dialogue with you, there's a problem. Say, "I feel like I'm talking too much. What is your take on what we've covered thus far?" My rule of thumb is that if I am speaking to VITO for sixty straight seconds, I have been speaking fifty seconds too long.

Honor the clock, no matter what. Stick to any prearranged time limit. If none has been established, then offer one, or ask, "How much time would you like to invest in this conversation/topic of interest?"

When asked, say how much it's going to cost. Count on this: Early on in your conversation, VITO will ask you, in no uncertain terms, what it is likely to cost to begin a business relationship with you. Have your answer ready, make sure it contains real numbers that are easy to understand, and be ready to deliver it in less than ten seconds. If you still need information to create a quote for VITO, say something like this: "On similar projects, the investments have ranged from $100,000 to $350,000. We will need to talk to some of your people to figure out where this project is going to fall on that scale."

Create mutual accountability. Specifically, never do anything for VITO without getting some kind of commitment in return. For instance, if you're going to do an analysis, and that analysis is going to take considerable work and resources, then you are within your rights to ask VITO to agree to do something specific with that analysis within a specific period of time. Not only are you within your rights on this point, your Equal Business Stature *depends* on your ability to ask VITO to be accountable, as in the example below.

You: "Ms. Importanta, my team of experts will complete their initial studies by the [end of the week], which means on [Monday] your CFO and COO will be able to confirm our deliverables. Would you make them available to my team for two hours no later than Wednesday with a brief meeting with you for no more than twenty minutes immediately thereafter?"

Ask VITO what should happen next. Never, ever end your first appointment without a firm plan and a clear commitment for mutual action items. Good questions for securing mutual accountability at the end of the first appointment include:

» "How should we move forward between now and March 1?"
» "How can we help with any [specifics]?"
» "What would you like me and [Justin Tyme, your COO] to do between now and the end of next week?"

If you have qualified the opportunity (see the previous chapter), and if VITO has orders for you, click your heels, salute, make an entry in your calendar, and get to work.

IMPORTANT!

Whenever VITO tells you to start work with the Decision Maker, then *tell VITO you will keep him or her in the loop* (do not ask permission to do this), and then *ask explicitly, with specific dates and times, for the opportunity to speak with VITO again before a final decision is made.* Nine times out of ten, VITO will agree to this.

If VITO simply asks *you* what should happen next, share your desired outcome.

Once You Get the Commitment for Your Second Appointment

Send a personalized, hand-signed thank-you note to both VITO and Tommie.

Your conversation with VITO is much more likely to go in-depth during your second appointment. I'll show you how to strategize for that first comprehensive conversation in the next chapter.

Chapter 22

In-Depth with VITO

If you play your cards right, you will, at some point, get more or less unrestricted talk time with VITO, either over the phone or in person. This meeting, which could go on for as long as (gasp!) twenty to thirty straight minutes, is most likely to happen as the result of a scheduled second appointment with VITO. Once you get that precious time, follow these guidelines.

Ask Good VITO Questions

There are five kinds of "good" questions to ask VITO during your in-depth appointment: open-ended, closed-ended (although these can be dangerous), clarifying, opinion, and social proof. Let's look at each now.

Open-Ended Questions
- » Cannot be answered with a simple "Yes" or "No"
- » Encourage VITO to reveal feelings about certain situations and therefore helps build rapport and Equal Business Stature
- » Typically begin with the words "when," "what," "how," "why," or "where"

For instance: "How does your organization typically move forward in making these types of decisions?"

Closed-Ended Questions

» Typically can be answered quickly with a simple "Yes" or "No" response
» Can be dangerous, as in, "Are you happy with your current supplier?" (What if VITO says, "Yes"?)
» Must be planned carefully. You need to know how you will deal with both possible responses from VITO.

 VITO RULE #30 Don't use more than one or two closed-ended questions during your entire conversation with VITO!

Clarifying Questions

» Ensure that you really understand what VITO is saying
» Give you the chance to express in your own words what VITO is trying to communicate
» Can, if used carefully, secure VITO's approval and prove that you have a good working knowledge of the topic under discussion

They typically sound like this:

"So, if I understand you correctly, (yada, yada, yada); is that right?"

"What I am hearing is that (yada yada yada), correct?"

Warning: Don't parrot back to VITO his or her *exact* words or phrases. This type of "questioning" is often perceived as condescending and unimaginative.

Opinion Questions

- » Reveal where VITO stands on any topic
- » Provide additional insight and information
- » Ensure that VITO is engaged in the conversation as an active participant
- » Show your esteem for VITO's position and experience
- » Stroke VITO's ego (which is never a bad thing)

For instance: "What's your opinion so far about how what we've been talking about fits in with the current economic climate your [industry] [company] is facing?"

Social Proof Questions

- » Establish your credibility on a certain topic
- » Illustrate to VITO that you have a certain level of experience with other high-level folks (i.e., CEOs, Presidents, Owners) in this VITO's industry

WARNING: Whenever you use a social proof question, you will want to avoid using any specific names of competitors (yours or VITO's). VITO may have just lost a big deal to that competitor! Instead, use what I call "relative ranking name dropping" in social proof questions. For example:

"The [CEO] of [one of the top five] [health care providers] was quoted as saying (yada, yada, yada). What's your opinion?"

Do Not Ask Stupid Questions!

Too many salespeople invest massive amounts of time, effort, and energy winning precious talk time with VITO only to lose the momentum (and the selling opportunity) by asking dumb-dumb questions like the following:

» "How's business?"
» "How's the economy affecting your business?"
» "How many employees do you have?"
» "What's your annual revenue?"

Questions like these serve as a flashing red light to VITO that says, "Hey, I didn't do my research; I'm bending over now, so please feel free to kick me out of your office as vigorously as possible."

Do the research and stay away from idiotic questions, and you won't feel the impact of VITO's foot on your (metaphorical) backside.

Remember the Basics

By now, you know the basics of communicating with VITO, but it's probably a good idea to remind yourself of them before the second appointment begins. Let VITO interrupt you. Offer solutions that address more than one problem. Follow VITO's lead. Don't do long, uninterruptable monologues. Offer a choice of several ideas and options.

Find Out: Which Brain Is VITO Using?

During your first in-depth discussion with VITO, it will be relatively easy to find out whether VITO is left- or right-brain dominant. One of these processing styles is almost certainly going to dominate your discussion, and you need to find out which it is.

VITOs who are left-brain driven like to discuss ideas in terms of logical connections using logic, words, lists, metrics, and so on.

VITOs who are right-brain driven are more inclined to relate to pictures, demos, imagination, experiences, and similarly hard-to-quantify experiences.

You can figure out which kind of VITO you're dealing with just by asking a few questions and really listening to the answers.

You: "VITO, when you selected CompetesWithMeCo, what criteria did you use?"

Left-brain dominant VITO: "We studied every consulting firm who specialized in the Asian market, ran the numbers, and it became immediately apparent that they were the best!"

Compare this to:

Right-brain dominant VITO: "One of our board members had a good experience with them. It just (looked/felt/sounded) like it was a good fit and it (looked/felt/sounded) like the right decision at that time."

Always Ask If It's Okay to Take Notes

This will flatter VITO a little bit, and it will also give you a written record of the discussion. Even if you're meeting with VITO over the phone, you should find some way to make sure that VITO knows you're writing everything down.

You: "VITO, would it be all right if I take notes?"

Suggest a Next Appointment

Always set up your desired next step/appointment before you start running short on time. For instance:

You: "Ms. Importanta, before we go any further, let's make sure we get this down on our calendars. If we get your [shipping invoices] by next [Thursday], we can have your proposal a week from that day, which means we can have our next meeting on [Friday] the [14th.] What time works best for you on that day?"

And, If You're Meeting in Person with VITO

Don't use an icebreaker!

VITOs hate these, and invariably look for a way to fast-forward over them. Every other salesperson can pretend they showed up to talk about golf; you know better. Get down to business. Remember this: Icebreakers are used to reduce tension. Question: Who's tense? Not VITO! Icebreakers are self-serving to the salesperson's needs and fears and have no place in any sales situation.

Don't be a space invader!

As you physically enter VITO's office, don't automatically make yourself at home. In most cultures, the "confidential zone" is the area within eighteen inches of everybody's body. This area is private and is meant to be occupied by invited guests only! (For instance, a spouse or "significant other" and one's close relatives.) The "individual zone" is the area between eighteen and thirty-two inches of everybody's body. This is where most of us feel comfortable with social and business interactions that involve individuals we already know. And the "sociable zone" is between thirty-two and forty-four inches of everybody's body. That's about the distance between VITO and you when you're sitting at VITO's desk. This distance is most comfortable for social and business interactions with individuals we don't yet know. The "common zone" is the area *beyond* forty-four inches, which is where most everyone is comfortable with initial contact involving brand-new acquaintances.

So, as you enter VITO's office, pause and wait to be invited in, and then wait to be shown where to sit. Once you take a seat, do not put anything on VITO's desk (like a product or a sample contract) without asking permission! In other words, don't move from the common zone to the confidential zone without being invited to do so!

Don't forget: You're on VITO time

Being on time for an in-person appointment with VITO means showing up ahead of time. Plan on getting to VITO, Inc. at least thirty minutes before your scheduled meeting! What will you do with that extra time? Here are a few ideas:

- » Notice whose name is on the employee of the month's parking space.
- » Read VITO, Inc.'s newsletter in the lobby.
- » Notice any plaques, trophies, or banners being displayed.
- » Read the most recent copy of VITO, Inc.'s annual report if there's one in the lobby.
- » Go to the washroom and freshen up.

Look sharp!

Make sure your appearance is neat, clean, and appropriate for the industry and company you're visiting. If you're in doubt, call ahead and ask the receptionist what the dress code is.

Bring a written agenda and review it with VITO

Yep, even if it's only for a ten-minute meeting. If you run out of time or you don't cover any items, you can easily put them on the agenda for your next appointment!

When VITO gives you his or her card, be sure to look at both sides of it

Very often, you will find VITO's mission statement on the backside. If it's there, make sure you take time to read it then and there and comment on it. If you're lucky, you may be able to pose a question like this: "Mr. Benefito, what exactly do you mean by excellence in customer relationships?" Listen carefully, because VITO will be telling you his or her expectations regarding personal treatment within this business relationship. (You can get similar insights from just about anything you read within VITO's mission statement.) When you're done reading VITO's card, put it in a silver or gold business-card holder. Never forget that VITO's business card is basically an extension of VITO's business, and, by extension, of VITO. Treat it with the respect it deserves.

A Final Thought about This Meeting: Three Options

If you appear to VITO to "own" your Equal Business Stature during this first in-depth discussion, you will be considered suitable for further interaction, and just about guaranteed another appointment.

If, for some reason, you appear to be of higher business stature than VITO, you will be admired and cultivated as a valuable contact.

If you appear to be of lower business stature, you will be tolerated by VITO, but kept at arm's length and most likely not be granted a second appointment.

Which will it be?

Chapter 23

Acquisition, Retention, and Winning Back

Do things always go the way we'd like with VITO? Of course not. There are some good reasons why VITO sales are lost, and some even better reasons to find a win inside that loss. This chapter gives you everything you need to know about acquisition, retention, and win-back strategies in the VITO sale.

Acquisition

Some salespeople don't have a clue about their cost of sales. They waste time prospecting for new business with unqualified organizations, stuck in endless meetings with individuals who live in Linoleumville. These salespeople spend most of their time spinning their wheels, wasting their own time and their organization's precious resources. At the end of a long protracted sales cycle, they have either little or nothing to show for it.

Current statistics show that (depending upon what's being sold) this ill-directed "prospecting" activity is costing the organization somewhere between $15,000 to a startling $250,000 per year for every salesperson who engages in it!

Retention

Some salespeople don't pay much attention to their existing customer base.

They infrequently and inconsistently touch base to see if budgets have been approved or whether any new projects are on the horizon. In the process, they'll take Seemore out to lunch or give him or her a pocket protector or some other logo-ized doo-dad, like a highlighter. This retention strategy (if you can call it that) leaves the seller vulnerable to VITO suddenly deciding to go to another vendor, and is actually costing the organization the lifetime value of *all* the accounts lost in this manner in a given year. Depending upon the size of the existing customer account that could, literally, be millions of dollars!

Win Back

Some salespeople don't spend any time at all making serious attempts to win back customers who have "voted with their feet" by hitting the high road and switching suppliers.

Current statistics show that chances of successfully winning back and selling to a former customer is 20–40 percent. That's significantly *higher* than the 5–20 percent chance you have of selling to a brand-new prospect. If you won back more customers, that would have a dramatic positive impact on your own (and your organization's) sales revenue number! If you want better commission checks, get better at winning your customers back!

This Is Your Sales Manager Calling

Imagine for a moment that your sales manager calls you into his or her office and says this:

"Will, we're going to give you a raise! Your salary will be $1.75 million. Flat. No bonus, no commissions, no trophies. You will, however, have to pay for all of the pre- and post-sales resources you use. All the admin support, all the photocopying, all the proposal prep, all the order entry, all the technical support, all the telephone calls, lunches, all the dinners, and all the logo-ized goodies that you give away. Oh, yeah—don't forget the joint sales calls you take me out on—you'll be billed for that, too. Whatever's left over, you get to keep. Lots of luck!"

My advice: Take the deal!

Here's why. I've spent most of this book on the process, tactics, skills, mindsets, and methods necessary to get an appointment with and sell to VITO. Once you know what VITO's hot buttons are and have a realistic plan for keeping VITO in the loop, you will find that a significant percentage of your "golden referrals" turn into revenue. You now have an acquisition model—and a highly cost-effective one at that!

Now we're going to learn how to keep VITO as a valued customer and win back any VITOs who may (for any number of reasons) have jumped ship! I'll also show you what to do when you're in a sales cycle and you've worked hard getting on the short list and in the bottom of the ninth inning with a tied score, full count, and bases loaded . . . you strike out! In my book, that's part of win back, too.

Retention of Existing Accounts

There are plenty of books and seminars around that will teach you "strategic account management," and I'm sure that one of those books or seminars is appropriate to your sales cycle, solution set, and marketplace. When you find it, though, I guarantee you that it won't cover what follows: *how to keep VITO actively involved in the expansion of the account.*

That, by the way, is the best way to achieve account retention: Keep your relationship with VITO strong, and keep VITO apprised of what's going on (and what could and should happen next) in your ever-expanding corner of VITO, Inc.

VITO RULE #31

The more time, energy, attention, and money VITO invests in the relationship with you, and the better you are at demonstrating to VITO the hard- and soft-dollar value your products, services, and solutions have actually delivered to VITO, Inc. in return for that investment, the less likely the account is to disconnect from you.

Take a look at how this might play out in one of the accounts you won *before* you started reading this book. Let me guess: You have a small foothold in this account. There are other opportunities for you to sell your stuff, but you're not doing it. Why? Because way back when you first sold the account, Seemore told you not to stray beyond the boundaries of Linoleumville. To get the business, you agreed. Here you sit with a thin slice of the total business. You're worried that you might not be able to retain the account, especially, if your competition gets to VITO first. What do you do?

First: Complete a value inventory that identifies the hard- and soft-dollar value of what you've been delivering. Don't scrimp on this. Do the research. Figure out what you've actually been delivering. *The better (as in more accurate and complete) your value inventory looks, the higher your chance of holding on to and growing this piece of* *business; the wimpier your value inventory, the less chance you'll hold on to and grow this account.*

Second: Compile a full evaluation of what "up-selling" can be done in this account. Estimate the amount of revenue (do this by product/service category if you sell more than one). Then estimate over what period of time all of this stuff can be sold.

Third: Find out VITO's name, Tommie's name, and VITO's phone number and e-mail address. (That's assuming you don't already have this information, of course.) Then get as much of the following information as you possibly can about this account's VITO:

> » What college/university did VITO graduate from?
> » What branch of the service did VITO serve in, if any?
> » Where did VITO grow up?
> » Where does VITO live now?
> » What philanthropic activities/endeavors is VITO involved in?
> » What hobbies does VITO enjoy?

(Here's a quick hint for answering the above questions: at a bare minimum, do a Google search on VITO's name and see what comes up. After you've done that, find out whether this VITO has an account on LinkedIn or Facebook.)

Fourth: Find out what competitor's products, services, and solutions VITO, Inc. is currently using in the areas where you want to up-sell.

Fifth: Find out whether VITO, Inc. has a board of directors; if it does, find out who sits on it. Once you know who's on the board of VITO, Inc., find out if any of the members are customers of yours.

Take all of this information and put it into a portfolio. Then make a photocopy of everything in the portfolio and put it into a separate file.

Now invest in another copy of *this book*. Hand carry it, along with your duplicate portfolio, to the highest-ranking executive in your organization who is or could be involved in the sales process. (Typically, that's the Director of Sales, the VP of Sales, the President, the CEO, and or the Owner).

After you've shared everything with your Director of Sales, VP of Sales, President, CEO, or Owner, ask that person to *call the VITO* in the account that you want to retain and grow. I shared this basic idea with you a little earlier in the book; here, I'm suggesting that you go the extra mile and arm your executive with all that cool information you gathered as part of your research. I'm also suggesting that you put a cool bookmark at the beginning of this chapter. Once your executive reads this, you'll have an ally on the VITO front in *your* camp!

Here's what your executive might say on that call to VITO:

Your Executive: "[Mr. Benefito], your team [Seemore Jones and Riley Getsitdone] and my team [Will Prosper] during the last [four years] have been helping you [increase shareholder value] while assisting in your efforts to reach [full compliance]. We suspect our efforts can be expanded to other areas of your organization. Before we begin to uncover all the possibilities, let's make sure we're meeting your expectations of a business partner."

VITO will most likely respond positively to that opening statement. As the conversation progresses, make sure your executive gets responses to the following questions/areas of importance:

» Are there any areas of unmet requirements in the current business relationship?
» Have there been any "unheard" complaints about the products, services, and solutions we are providing?
» Is there anything that VITO or any of the Decision Makers would like to see improved, changed, or realigned?

> » What, if anything, would VITO like to see added to the existing business relationship?

Granted, VITO may not know the answers to all of these questions, but VITO will know where you should go to get the answers.

Once your executive has raised all of these issues, he or she should say something like this:

Your Executive: "We strongly suspect that we could assist in further increasing [efficiencies and effectiveness] in your [shipping and receiving, accounting, operations, and marketing departments]. How would you suggest our teams move forward in the next [30] days to quickly uncover all of the possibilities?"

Granted, there's more to the conversation depending upon how VITO responds, but you get the drift.

Winning Back a Lost Customer

Most companies don't have a win-back program in place. This is a tragedy! With a little work, a percentage of your lost business can be recaptured, but you've got to be ready, willing, and able to eat a little bit of humble pie in the process. Look at the list of action items that follow, each of which will help you increase your odds of winning this piece of business back. (That's what you want to do, right?)

Connect (or Reconnect) with VITO and:

1. Offer both a verbal *and* a written apology for whatever problems arose in the account.
2. Ask in a very sincere way, "What can we do to win back your business?" and or "Who can we talk with to find out exactly why you decided to switch?"

3. After you find out the answers to 2, make sure you fully communicate the changes you've made in writing. Then ask VITO
   if that's enough to earn the business back.

After that comes the hard part! *Stay in touch;* don't just make one
attempt at the win back.

When a customer does come back, make it easy and painless.
Avoid any "I told you so" or "I knew you'd be back" vibe.

Once you're successful at the win back, make damn sure you don't
lose this business again!

The Magic Words

Once you get the ball rolling in any of the three modes we've discussed
in this chapter—acquisition, retention, or win back—give yourself an
"insurance policy" by posting this question to VITO:

You: "Ms. Importanta, in the next [several weeks], your team and
our experts will be working together to discover if what we suspect is
possible can actually take place inasmuch as [increasing shareholder
value] while achieving [full compliance] is a major priority for you.
I have a personal favor to ask of you (pause for a quick moment):
Whatever their findings and decisions are, whether for or against
starting a business relationship with my organization, would you
grant me the privilege of an in-person visit with you?"

Then, if you ever need to play your get-out-of-jail-free card—*play it!*

Chapter 24

The VITO Zone

Meeting with VITO, and selling to VITO, is, first and foremost, a state of mind. If you're regularly in touch with your inner VITO, then you're regularly going to be "in the zone," and you're going to find it very easy to consistently implement what I've shared with you in this book. You're also going to find it very easy to maintain momentum throughout the sales cycle. On the other hand, if you're not in the zone, what I've shared with you is unlikely to produce a permanent zip code in Sales Heaven.

Over the years, I've come up with some specific ideas for staying in the mindset that makes good conversations with VITO happen, accelerates your time to win, and gets you lots of repeat business from VITO. My favorite tactics for staying in this essential zone—that I call the VITO Zone—appear in this chapter.

Seven Simple Ways to Stay in the VITO Zone

How many of these seven VITO rules can you put to use *this week*?

After a good call with VITO, call another VITO
immediately.

Rearrange your schedule to take advantage of the adrenaline rush you get right after a great connection with VITO. There is no greater time to win an appointment with a new prospective VITO than immediately after you hang up the phone from another VITO conversation that's gone well.

VITO RULE #33

Use what works; avoid what doesn't.

Closely analyze each and every call you have with VITO or Tommie. Figure out what went right and repeat whatever that was. Figure out what went wrong and stay away from whatever that was. This is a classic VITO trait. Winners look for clues after each great outcome and each disappointing outcome, and then use those clues intelligently. It's never luck that gets you an outcome, positive or negative. Winning always leaves a trail of actions that can be followed again and again. Real winners are "consciously competent"—they know why they succeed. When they fail, they want to know why that happened, too. Get into the habit of asking your customer VITOs (and Tommies) what worked as well as what didn't work in your initial approach. Never stop doing this! Make your approach to VITO one of continuous improvement.

Set goals that are doable.

I've been asked may times: "How many VITO letters do I need to send each week?" My answer is always the same, regardless of the industry or the product, service, or solution being sold: "Don't send any more than you can effectively follow up on, but *do* send enough that you are taking action every day."

By taking action on a daily basis, you'll accomplish three very important steps.

1. You'll be filling your forecast with qualified VITO opportunities. That's good!
2. You'll be getting into a VITO prospecting habit for the long term. That's even better. Research shows that if you take action on a specific task for twenty-one days or longer, it will become habit. That's also good!
3. You'll be refining your approach and becoming more comfortable and confident with the process as time goes on. That's even better!

VITO RULE

#35 Reward yourself after each accomplishment.

You're no fool, and neither is your brain! If you work hard at doing anything, and you actually accomplish the goal but forget to reward yourself, beware! You're sending a message to your brain: "Work hard, and I'll expect you to work even harder!" Your brain doesn't dig that.

After just a short while of this all-work-and-no-play treatment, your brain gets tired, and without you even knowing it, starts to sabotage itself . . . and you! Get in the habit of rewarding yourself for each and every goal you meet or exceed. The reward can be just about anything. For example, every time I finished a chapter of this book, I rewarded myself with a surf session. Although I surf a lot, these reward sessions were special. As I sat on my board waiting for the next wave, I felt bigger and better about myself because I had done exactly what I set out to do. You will, too!

VITO RULE #36 Make promises to yourself and others.

I find now that I actually prefer making promises to myself and other people over setting goals. This is because my brain is better at keeping promises than it is at attaining goals. I bet yours is, too. Ask yourself these two questions:

1. Over the past nine months, how many goals have I set and actually accomplished?
2. Over the past nine months, how many promises have I made to myself and kept?

See what I mean?

VITO RULE #37 Remember: Your ultimate accountability lies in implementing what you learn.

Take personal responsibility for implementing the good stuff I've shared with you, and leave the results to the Universe. You can't take responsibility for what you can't control. However, you can take something you have *no* control over and then use that as an excuse to avoid learning and improving in some area of your life. For instance:

» "I tried something like this before and it didn't work."
» "I knew VITO wouldn't take my call."
» "I've left a voice mail message and got no return call. This is a waste of time."
» "What's the use? I got shunted to Seemore anyway."

Yes, I realize it is easier to play the blame game than it is to stay *in* the game. The VITO mindset, however, rejects this easy way out. The VITO mindset demands that you ask, "What did I *learn* from this? How can I *use* what I learned next time?" That's the ultimate accountability!

> **VITO RULE**
> **#38** Have a positive attitude.

Yeah, yeah—you've heard it all before, and you still have to take out the garbage twice a week. Guess what, though? Once you spend enough time with VITOs, you realize this popular piece of advice is much easier to carry out than most people think! You really can create and sustain a positive attitude by taking four simple steps each and every day. (I learned the four steps from my friend, Dr. Denis Waitley, one of the most listened-to voices in the world for self-improvement.)

1. Stop watching the news before you go to bed.
2. Stop waking up to an alarm set to the morning traffic report.
3. Stop listening to, reading, or hanging around with any individual, person, or group who is negative in any way.
4. Start each day and end each day with a thankful thought for all that you have in life.

It works for me. It works for VITO. And it might just work for you!

Chapter 25

The Holy Grail

I've been teaching people how to use this system for about a quarter-century now. It's only with the publication of this book, and the completion of this chapter, that I've reached what I consider the "Holy Grail"—the be-all and end-all goal—when it comes to summarizing and reinforcing the VITO material in written form.

Let's start with an obvious point: Salespeople usually don't have a lot of extra time on their hands. That's why I've tried to keep the chapters in this book short. Most of them can be read easily and thoroughly during a lunch break!

That time problem brings us to this chapter. My big problem with books about selling is that so many of them don't offer a tight, well-designed "road map" that gives an overview of the big ideas that drive the entire process. What happens if you need a quick refresher on a key point or advice on where you can get details on a specific area of the system where you're drawing a blank? Too often, the answer is, "Read the book again."

I've designed this book differently, because I know most salespeople (including yours truly) don't have time for that. Next, you will find *all* the core VITO Rules you have learned in previous chapters.

This is the road map of the philosophy I have shared with you in this book. Photocopy it and hang it in your cubicle! (The lawyers tell me that's okay as long as you're doing it for your own personal use.)

After each VITO Rule, you'll find a page reference that will point you toward a fuller discussion of the VITO principle in question.

Don't just READ these VITO Rules—post them and INTER-NALIZE THEM, so you can find your own Holy Grail of Selling!

VITO Rule Zero: *(This is the foundation rule from which every other VITO RULE is derived!) VITO is the ultimate approver of everything that happens in the organization, including your sale.*

(See page 5.)

VITO Rule 1: *VITO will like me because I am like VITO.*

(See page 16.)

VITO Rule 2: *VITO will like what my product can do for him or her because it's in alignment with what VITO wants.*

(See page 16.)

VITO Rule 3: *I am measured at my job as a salesperson in a way that's similar to how VITO is measured at the job of Very Important Top Officer.*

(See page 16.)

VITO Rule 4: *Because time is so valuable, VITOs don't treat all potential business relationships equally, and neither should you.*

(See page 19.)

VITO Rule 5: *When you fly with VITO, everybody else in the organization follows!*
(See page 24.)

VITO Rule 6: *Be accountable for your own sales process.*
(See page 24.)

VITO Rule 7: *A process isn't a process unless you can replicate it.*
(See page 35.)

VITO Rule 8: *Above every Decision Maker, and above every decision in the enterprise, sits VITO—the approver of the sale and everything else.*
(See page 42.)

VITO Rule 9: *No matter what anyone else in the buying enterprise has to say about some salesperson's offering, VITO can (and often will) kill that offering on a moment's notice.*
(See page 45.)

VITO Rule 10: *VITO's Decision Makers get paid to say yes.*
(See page 54.)

VITO Rule 11: *Influencers can't buy jack. Never could. Never would. Never will. Period. End of story.*
(See page 57.)

VITO Rule 12: *Follow the perfect sales process.*
(See page 63.)

VITO Rule 13: *Like VITO, you have to be willing to change course as circumstances demand in order to hit your goal.*

(See page 66.)

VITO Rule 14: *What matters is not the title, but the traits you share with VITO.*

(See page 72.)

VITO Rule 15: *Selling to VITO (also known as picking up the phone and calling VITO) is marketing, advertising, public relations, and sales all at the same time!*

(See page 83.)

VITO Rule 16: *When you create any written correspondence that you want VITO to actually process, you'll have to make it a fast read. A fast read in VITO's world means thirty seconds.*

(See page 92.)

VITO Rule 17: *VITOs are looking for ways to improve every area of their organization, not just the area you happen to know about and are working with.*

(See page 101.)

VITO Rule 18: *You must know which VITOs to approach . . . and which not to approach.*

(See page 104.)

VITO Rule 19: *You must know how to approach VITO.*

(See page 107.)

VITO Rule 20: *Every piece of VITO correspondence has six specific parts, each of which must stand on its own but also be logically connected to all the other parts.*

(See page 109.)

VITO Rule 21: *It's okay to make mistakes . . . because none of this is life threatening.*

(See page 126.)

VITO Rule 22: *Once you complete all eight of the precorrespondence steps, and not before, you will be ready to send your VITO correspondence.*

(See page 143.)

VITO Rule 23: *When interacting with the Receptionist Gatekeeper, you must close with the words, "Thank you!" spoken briskly and confidently!*

(See page 146.)

VITO Rule 24: *When talking with Tommie, forget that VITO exists!*

(See page 149.)

VITO Rule 25: *The tone, modulation, and pacing of your voice will determine how easy or difficult it is for VITO to listen to (and act on!) your message.*

(See page 154.)

VITO RULE 26: *Be ready for all of the six good things that can happen during a call to VITO.*

(See page 161.)

VITO Rule 27: *You will inevitably be shunted to the person within VITO, Inc. whom you sound the most like.*
(See page 167.)

VITO Rule 28: *Do not accept shunts from unqualified opportunities!*
(See page 174.)

VITO Rule 29: *Know what you want from the meeting.*
(See page 178.)

VITO Rule 30: *Don't use more than one or two closed-ended questions during your entire conversation with VITO!*
(See page 184.)

VITO Rule 31: *The more time, energy, attention, and money VITO invests in the relationship with you, and the better you are at demonstrating to VITO the hard- and soft-dollar value your products, services, and solutions have actually delivered to VITO, Inc. in return for that investment, the less likely the account is to disconnect from you.*
(See page 194.)

VITO Rule 32: *After a good call with VITO, call another VITO immediately.*
(See page 200.)

VITO Rule 33: *Use what works; avoid what doesn't.*
(See page 200.)

VITO Rule 34: *Set goals that are doable.*
(See page 200.)

VITO Rule 35: *Reward yourself after each accomplishment.*
(See page 201.)

VITO Rule 36: *Make promises to yourself and others.*
(See page 202.)

VITO Rule 37: *Remember: Your ultimate accountability lies in implementing what you learn.*
(See page 202.)

VITO Rule 38: *Have a positive attitude.*
(See page 203.)

Don't stop here! Make sure you register for your free month in my exclusive Club VITO! Turn to page 231 for my web address and easy-to-follow instructions!

Appendix A

The Template of Ideal Prospects (TIP) and the Benefit Matrix

A "Tip" You Can Count On!

When completed, this exercise will provide you with vital information that will assist you in qualifying new prospects before and during the first sales call. Your template of ideal Prospects (TIP) will help you compare your best customers to new prospects—and show you where your best opportunities lie.

Start by identifying your very best existing customers! Once you have created this list, you must find answers to the key questions in the following categories and record them in a notebook or data file.

Basic company data. What distinguishes this company from others who are not as good a "fit" with your organization? In the distribution industry, for example, you might list: number of parts in inventory; season needs; purchasing habits on critical components; shipping unit size; order origin and entry procedures (processed from catalog? counter? telephone?); fleet owned or leased; number of employees; annual revenue; number of salespeople; etc.

Relevant sales parameter data. Determine specific problems solved through use of your product or service; third-party "value-added" products or services necessary to secure the sale; price sensitivity among key decision makers; your price position among competitors; and titles of key contacts.

Tangible and intangible benefits. Highlight the specific, quantifiable benefits this customer is realizing as a result of using your solution and having a business relationship with your company.

That's What Your Happy Customer Looks Like

There will be some exceptions, but generally, prospects with profiles that show extreme differences from those of your best customer(s) should be avoided on placed on the far back burner. While it is not necessary for you to do exhaustive research in preparation for a call on a new prospect, you may do so if you wish. It is essential, though, to have a strong sense of the profile of your *current* satisfied customers and to be ready to "fill in the blanks" of your templates as your learn more about new opportunities.

Here's a sheet you can use to record your TIP criteria . . . and evaluate prospects against those criteria.

INDUSTRY:		
Profile: Best Customer	**Profile: This Prospect**	**Match?**

Notes:

Benefits:

If you want to get the electronic version of this, all you need to do is sign up for your free membership in Club VITO/Quota Busters. See page 229 in this book!

Appendix B

Finding VITO, Tracking VITO

Caution: If you flipped to this page before reading the twenty-five main chapters of this book, little of what you're about to read will make any sense whatsoever.

Finding VITO

You know as well as I do it's easier today than it's ever been to find the names of prospects. There is no shortage of websites that you can use to get your first 100 or so contact names for free, sign up for, subscribe to or figure out how to pirate. The questions that arise about such a list, though, include:

- » How good is the list?
- » How fresh is it?
- » How many other people have gotten their hot little hands on it?
- » Most importantly, how will *you* use it?

Here's what you'll need to do.

Step One

Make sure you complete your TIP (Template of Ideal Prospects), which you'll find in Appendix A. Armed with the names of the industries that you'll be prospecting, you must then find the relevant company names that match up with your template. To do that, you must move to . . .

Step Two

Go on line and find any and all organizations and or associations that support the industries that you identified in Step One. Contact them and find out who the largest member organizations are.

Now use any of the following free and fee ways to find out the names of companies and VITO's name:

» *www.Google.com*
» *www.wikianswers.com*
» *www.Dunn&Bradstreet.com*
» *www.Hoovers.com*
» *www.edgar.org*
» *www.selectory.com*

Tracking VITO

I really don't care much for Customer Relationship Management (CRM) software packages. They're really not about Customer Relationships at all. They're mostly about keeping track of what we salespeople are doing (or not doing). In the table below you'll find what I use to keep track of my VITO calls. At the end of any day of calling I can easily measure my performance, effectiveness, and efficiency.

My personal goals are:

1. Up to a 30 percent direct contact (conversation) with VITO
2. Up to a 35 percent direct contact (conversation) with VITO's Personal Assistant
3. Up to a 35 percent direct contact with VITO's Voice Mail system
4. Up to a 50 percent shunt rate to the proper Decision Maker (only after I complete my first call objectives).

Here's the sheet I use to keep track of that information, one company at a time.

Company Name	
VITO Name Title	
VITO's Tele #	
VITO's P/A's Name	
VITO Conversation	(Y/N)
VITO's P/A Conversation	(Y/N)
Voicemail Message	(Y/N)
Shunt to Decision Maker	(Y/N)
Completed First-Call Objectives?	(Y/N)
Appointment Set	(Y/N) Date/Time:
Next Steps	
Thank you note	
Send additional information	

Simple, isn't it? If you want to get the electronic version of this, you'll find it after all you need to do is you sign up for your Free membership in Club VITO/Quota Busters. See page 229 in this book!

Appendix C

Social Media and VITO

Back in the day (you know, the pre-2000 day) you had to connect with VITO in one of three ways: the telephone, the printed word, or good old face-to-face conversation. Nowadays, you have at least three powerful online tools in your arsenal. The good news is that you can use all three of these tools—each of which falls under the category of *social media*—both as a resource for good pre-call information on VITO and VITO Inc., *as well as* a means for communicating with VITO and his/her direct reports after you make initial contact. Why not take advantage?

Each of these social media platforms could itself could easily be the subject of a book; this isn't that book. I'm working on the assumption that you are looking for a concise overview of the best ways to use the tool in question. There are plenty of other important social media sites you should visit. The ones listed below are just the most three indispensable for businesspeople—in my view, anyway. *Even if you don't consider yourself an "online person," you owe it to yourself to set up an account in each of these three spaces.*

Twitter

Twitter (*www.twitter.com*) gives you, and VITO, the opportunity to share whatever seems important at the moment.

But there's a catch: What's important at any given moment can be no longer than 140 text characters long. This paragraph would just fit.

Get the idea? As a pre-call research tool, Twitter is best described as "hit-or-miss" . . . but boy, when you hit, do you ever hit. Once you set up your account, you can easily do a search for any VITO whose name you've uncovered. If the VITO you're after happens to have a Twitter account (and more and more of them do these days), you can "follow" that VITO, whether you know him or her personally or not, and get a direct feed of VITO's "tweets" (i.e., 140-character-or-less musings). That gives you all VITO's latest brilliant ideas, pet peeves, favorite articles, thoughts on changes in his/her industry, and, if you're lucky, major business goals. Sound like something you might want to build a VITO letter around? I thought so. (Of course, you may also get links to VITO's favorite casserole recipes.)

You can also send your own "tweets"—the trick here is getting people to decide to "follow" you so that you have someone to share your pearls of wisdom with. These concise message can't come off as "sales-y," and must be based on your own or your company's area of expertise. Needless to say, you'll want to keep your Twitter posts crisp and professional. Don't worry about sending a message every ten minutes; shoot for two or three times a week.

Facebook

Facebook (*www.facebook.com*) has effectively become the town square of the on-line era. It's where you interact with people. In the (increasingly unlikely) event that you haven't yet encountered Facebook, I'll limit my remarks to the bare facts: You can use this amazingly easy-to-master interface to add friends and send them messages, update your personal profile so that it reflects what's happening in your world, and notify friends about interesting things you've found on-line (or anywhere else). Additionally, users can join networks organized by city, workplace, and school or college. The site also offers a series of popular socially driven online games.

Like Twitter, Facebook is highly addictive. Unlike Twitter, it offers a vast array of applications and activities, all of which help you interact with other people. The Facebook world takes a little longer to master, but it's still amazingly easy to use and designed to help you amass a large list of friends in a short time. Why not harness that power on behalf of your emerging relationship with VITO?

One word of caution: It's very easy to blur personal and business lines on Facebook. Make sure you keep the two worlds separate.

LinkedIn

LinkedIn (*www.linkedin.com*) is, unlike Twitter and Facebook, intended for business networking. It takes a little longer to set up your account than it does to set up a Facebook account, but the rewards are hard to overstate. As of this writing, both Twitter and Facebook are free; technically, LinkedIn is, too, but there are advanced search features you'll probably decide are worth the (modest) additional fee. It's likely that an important Decision Maker at VITO, Inc., possibly VITO himself or herself, has a page on LinkedIn. If you don't know what's on it, you should. (Given how many professionals are using LinkedIn for personal and company marketing purposes—60 million at last count—assume that your competition already *does* know what's on that page.)

Appendix D

Your Prospecting Ratio

It's amazing how for the most part "formulas" are timeless, especially when they are proven in the field. In this appendix we'll look at what you will need to use to forecast your own sales targets on a daily basis as part of your selling to VITO sales work. Don't leave this work to your sales manager, your CRM system, or any other automated process. Take control of your own career and monitor your own VITO prospecting ratios!

Definitions

A VITO *suspect* is a company that fits your Template of Ideal Prospects (see Appendix A) and that is within the territory you've been assigned.

A VITO *prospect* is a suspect you've contacted (at the VITO and/or Decision Maker level) who has needs similar to those you have met successfully in other accounts.

A VITO *hot lead* is a prospect who will give you an equal shot at winning the business, someone you could win within the context of your normal sales cycle. Typically, you have met with VITO and/ or one or more Decision Makers, looked at the mutual opportunities, and given at least an overview of your products, services, and solutions.

Step One: Targets

Monitor your own sales work for one month (or whatever period is appropriate in your industry) and answer these questions:

If you contacted 100 suspects (via telephone calls, mailings, in-person meetings, or a combination of these), how many prospects would result?
Write your answer here: (A) _____

How many of the prospects identified in (A) would turn into "hot leads" you would be able to develop a detailed proposal for?
Write your answer here: (B) _____

How many of the hot leads you identified in (B) would you turn into actual sales?
Write your answer here: (C) _____

Step Two: Ratio

Divide the number on line C by 100. The result is your ratio.
Write your answer here: (R) _____

Step Three: Goals

What is your yearly quota or sales goal, in dollars?
(I) _____

What are your projected sales totals, in dollars, from current customers?
(II) _____

Subtract Item II from Item I to yield the amount of new sales dollars needed this year
(III) _____

Enter the dollar amount of your average sale.
(IV) _____

Divide Item III by Item IV to yield the number of new sales needed this year.
(V) _____

Step Four: Task

Divide the number in item V by your ratio (Line R in Step Two).
Write your answer here: _____

This is the number of new VITO suspects you need to contact in the coming year to reach your yearly target. Divide that number by 52, unless you plan on taking a week or two of vacation! and you'll know how many suspects you must contact each week to make your quota.

Note: Aim high! I always shoot for 125 percent of quota if I want to hit 110 percent!